WILLIAM of MALMESBURY'S
Life of Saint WULSTAN

WILLIAM of MALMESBURY'S
Life of Saint WULSTAN

Rendered into English by
J. H. F. PEILE
Archdeacon of Worcester

First published in 1934.
Facsimile reprint 1996
Llanerch Publishers,
Felinfach.

Copyright ©
J.H.F. Peile, 1934,
Mrs G. Aldridge, 1996.

ISBN 1 86143 025 6

PREFACE

THIS translation is taken from the Latin *Vita Wulfstani* of William of Malmesbury which is itself a version (made between 1124 and 1143) of the English *Life* by the monk Coleman, Wulstan's friend and Chaplain who wrote it after Wulstan's death in 1095 and himself died in 1113. No copy of Coleman's work is known to exist: but it is conjectured that it went to Rome at the time of Wulstan's canonisation, and may yet be discovered in the archives of the Vatican—*The Vita Wulfstani* was edited for the Royal Historical Society in 1928 by Mr R. R. Darlington, and I shall have done some service if my little book sends readers back to this edition. I cannot easily overstate my indebtedness to Mr Darlington both for his admirable Introduction, Text, and Notes, and for his great kindness in reading through my manuscript and making valuable suggestions.

My obligation to Mr Darlington being acknowledged, I would add that for any pleasure or profit the reader may derive from my version of the Life of Wulstan he has mainly to thank that learned and diligent researcher in the early history of the Cathedral and Priory, Sir Ivor Atkins, who practically insisted on my attempting the task, and has taken endless trouble in arranging for its publication.

Worcester, September 1934.

The LIFE of S. WULSTAN

⁋ Here begins William of Malmesbury's letter to the Brethren of Worcester.

CHAPTER I

TO the venerable Lord Prior Warin and to the whole reverend convent of Worcester, William sends the love of a son, the respect of a servant. It is long since you laid your commands on me to set my hand to a life of our holy father Wulstan, and for awhile I have shirked the task. I had many reasons—but the first and greatest was that, conscious of my unworthiness, I am taking upon me a work beyond my strength in praising the Saint. *Praise hath no comeliness in the mouth of a sinner.* Moreover, the power of your commands was lessened by a fear that, in obeying them, I should incur the ill-will of some by thrusting myself upon a task hitherto untried, and better left to a better man. These fears would have bridled my tongue with a stubborn silence, but that a hope inspired by the goodness of the blessed Bishop gave me courage and consolation. It was blessed Wulstan's way to forgive the offences of those who only spoke their love for him, and to defend them with his protection as with a shield. How much more then will he pardon one who is meditating a whole written book about him, and not fail to enrich his language. Our Lord Christ too will deign to turn aside envy from this work, undertaken as it is, not in the pride of learning but in the service of true devotion. Wherefore, my brethren, trusting in his help, I will do your bidding. Timid delay shall no longer cloud my purpose, but swift accomplishment shall atone for past slowness. And you, while you live, shall know right well that I say nothing that does not rest on solid truth, and is found in the witness of men worthy of belief. The older among you have seen with their eyes; the younger have heard with their ears. But for them that come after, when the memory of the things done shall grow cold, doubts may arise, unless I bring forth a strong witness. Therefore, seeing that the acts of Saints must needs be right faithfully recorded, I give no doubtful surety of what I say. My surety is your monk Coleman, a man of no little learning, and well skilled in his native tongue. He wrote in English that the memory of the things done should not vanish away: and his Life of the said father, if you look to the sense, pleases and informs; if you look to the letter, it is rude and simple enough. Coleman deserves the fullest credence: for as a disciple he knew his master's ways closely: as his chaplain for fifteen years he knew his religion. So, as you desired, I have kept close to Coleman's Life, making no change in the order of events, altering nothing in the true relation of facts. But in setting down what Wulstan said, or might on occasion have said, I have used my own judgment, always with careful regard for truth. A man who has abundance of time, and enjoys his own faculty of expression, may be allowed, when he has the facts certain, to deal more freely with speeches, except those which for their excellent radiance require to be briefly recorded. Accordingly I beg you to grant me this favour: protect my little work from envious rivals: and commend my offering and service to the most pious Wulstan, as you can, being in Worcester: venerable lords and worthily beloved fathers.

Here ends the letter.

¶ The prologue begins.

IN the holy Scriptures are many things, or as I hold things without number, whereby the divine mercy directs the minds of mortal men to the practice of a good life, both precepts and examples. By those they are taught how they ought to live; by these it is conveyed how easy it is by the help of God to do what is commanded. In some men Nature has implanted this mind, that, although they know both are needful, yet they love rather to hear examples than exhortation. And to the deeds of men of old time they pay the respect due to antiquity: but they are taken with a keener pleasure if the life of some Saint who lived but now is set forth, in which they may behold as in a glass, thus to speak, a living image of religion: for the newness adds pleasantly to the story—so that no one need lose hope that he himself may be enabled by God's grace to accomplish what he hears has been done so lately by another. Hence I account not unworthy the desire which has arisen in my mind not to grudge to posterity a Life of blessed Wulstan, Bishop of Worcester: but with my pen, such as it is, to commend it to undying memory. For here was a man akin to our own times, and yet in virtue not unlike the early fathers. So I promise to the kind reader great gain: namely that although he look up to him no less than to the ancients for the glory of his miracles, yet, seeing that he lived but a little while since, the reader may strive to follow his way of life with emulous feet. Not indeed that I say this to claim for many this blessedness that they shall be able to imitate Wulstan as Wulstan was an imitator of Christ. Nay rather the few whom Jesus loves shall be able, seeing him as it were far before them, to press on in the steps of his virtues, rather than to engrave those virtues perfectly in their own hearts. To such a degree (I speak with all reverence for the older saints) did he fall short of none of them in his mastery over vices— to such a degree did he carry the love of virtue which he conceived as a child with good success to old age. Wherefore it had been but just that the writer of his deeds should be a man of polished speech and proved learning, in order that sublime actions should not be set forth in mean language, and the praises should follow the pattern of what he praised. For me, I have not the skill of the orator, nor does my conscience approve the innocence of my life. Only obedience constrains me not stubbornly to refuse a task which the call of my brethren lays upon me, a task moreover which I am pledged to fulfil, and one which is profitable to my soul. May the mercy of the Holy Spirit be with me that my pen may be guided by the inspiration of Him by whose power Wulstan abounded in welldoing. Those who strive to excel in the art of rhetoric

The Prologue

thus order their discourses: first they secure the good will of the hearer—next they win his attention—and last they have him ready to be instructed. This manner of speaking when the matter demands it I do not neglect. But here such rhetorical devices are beside the mark. It is superfluous to seek for arguments where faith calls us to believe, and the subject invites us to read. I think Wulstan will never lack for readers so long as the stars turn about the pole, and there is any writing in the world. Such favour among men did he establish for himself by the mercy of God while he lived—and still holds after death.

But I have drawn out my preface long enough. Now, trusting in the help of heaven I will begin the task I have undertaken.

Here ends the Prologue.

☫ Here begins the life of Saint Wulstan, Bishop and Confessor.

IN the parts of Mercia lies the famous Shire of Warwick—and there in a village called Itchington. Here the house of venerable Wulstan had dwelt from the third and the fourth generation. His father was named Æthelstan, his mother Wulfgifu, of no mean birth or estate: so using the world that they might render to God the things that are God's. To the things of this world they gave little care, much to the things of God. In them diligence so vied with goodness that the one supplied the means, the other the love of virtuous action. The fruit of their pure wedded love was a son who was to prove the glory of England. The boy was called Wulstan, a name taken in the former part from his mother's, in the latter from his father's. With happy omen the hopeful child borrowed from the name of either parent to draw in to himself the holiness of each, and, methinks, marvellously to surpass it. Surely their memory would utterly have perished, had not their son's shining holiness set it on high in the sight of men. Wulstan was first taught his letters at Evesham —then his tender mind was trained in more perfect learning at Peterborough. It is pleasant to tell how even then he gave abundant proofs of the virtues which lay hid in him; such ripeness, such holiness in thought and speech did the promising boy's modesty express. Fasting, in so far as his age allowed, he did not neglect: he offered up humble prayers to heaven. Foolish talking, which is the fuel of temptation, he checked, first in himself then in others. So quickly did he increase in wisdom that he brought together boys of his own age, and even some that were older, in earnest prayer that by living well they might form in themselves an image of the good life. If he did wrong, he bade them tell him of it, and gladly yielded himself to correction. With him good desires were brought to good effect, for he saw nothing worthy of imitation that he did not adopt as an example. By so doing he showed clearly that he was a wise boy, and would be a wise man: according to what the divine wisdom has woven into the writings of Solomon, '*Rebuke a wise man and he will love thee.*' No less did he by nature seize for himself what Philosophy of old gave forth from its inmost shrine—*Ever set before the eyes of the mind some good man the thought of whom may order thy thoughts and actions. He will not easily depart from righteousness who is ever pondering on some God or man whose fear will keep him back from wrong-doing.*

At that time Wulstan had to his master one Erwin, a man skilled in writing and in making pictures of what he would. He had lent to young Wulstan two books, a sacramentary and a psalter in which he had illuminated the capitals with gold. The boy was delighted with the marvel of the enriched letters—and while his eager eyes dwelt on the beauty of the colours, his mind was drinking in the meaning of the text. But his teacher, looking to this world's profit, and hoping for a greater reward, gave the sacramentary to Cnut who was then king, and the psalter to his Queen Emma. The boy was heartbroken at the loss, and sighed bitterly. Sorrow brought slumber: and as he slept, behold a man with the face of an angel dispelled his sadness, and promised that he should have the books again—and so it came to pass, but long after, as will appear in my story. So childhood's spring-time passed, and Wulstan increasing as in stature so in holiness put on young manhood as a garment. Yet he did not, as so often befalls in that time of life, suffer any spot to defile his chastity—but bore the palm of virginity unstained to heaven. There was with him in all things abundance of the grace of God, that the freedom of his will might not be shaken. He felt from the beginning the gift of chastity poured into him from above: and he did not suffer any peevish silence to prevent him from confessing it: but ungrudgingly offered to others the heavenly nectar of which he himself had drunk. How it came to pass I will tell, that generations to come may understand what a measure of God's grace did both prevent and follow Wulstan in his youth. When he was returned from Peterborough to his parents, a damsel of the neighbourhood set herself to make shipwreck of his modesty and tempt him to sinful pleasures. She would ever be pressing his hand, beckoning with her eyes, and tempting him with wanton gestures which foretell the death of virginity. But when Wulstan's natural chastity made all her shameless desires vain, she still pursued him as is now set down. A great company of young men was met in a field. What their favourite sport was, I cannot tell. But doubtless there were races on the level sward: the air rang with the cries of the bystanders encouraging the runners. Wulstan shone out among the rest—and by common consent bore off the prize. The rustic throng shouted his praises, and re-echoed them again and again. Another might have rejoiced in these songs of victory—and his heart might have swelled high with the breath of applause. But neither by look nor in thought did Wulstan acknowledge their praises. So the devil was beaten there; and tried another way of assault. He put it into the heart of the damsel aforesaid, who was standing by, to approach. She, nothing loth, began to dance before Wulstan with lascivious movements apt to take the eyes of a lover. And he, whom touches and glances had not moved, yielded to her seductive gestures, and panted with desire. But in a moment he came to a better mind, and burst into tears:

and took flight into rough thickets and thorny places. There he lay a little way off, while the others went on with their games. And as he still pondered, and accused himself of many sins, sleep came upon him, and a miracle was seen. For a calm and bright cloud came down from above, deceiving the eyes of the beholders. Straightway the brightness of the cloud dispersed the mists of folly: and the wanton minds of the young men were sobered. They ran in haste to the spot, and came to Wulstan, anxiously enquiring what that sign should mean. He would not hide anything from them; and, that the flame of divine love which had shone upon him might cast its rays upon his fellows, he told them the whole matter as it had befallen. Of late, he said, I was burning fiercely with the desire of the flesh—now, watered with divine dew I am cool through all my being. I hope that henceforth I shall be free from the prickings of the flesh, and by the help of God's mercy no longer troubled. The word was prophetic, and was fulfilled in the event. Never from that day forth did any marvel of beauty attract his mind or his eye; and his sleep was not broken by ill dreams. Coleman said he had learned this from Hemming the Subprior, who declared he had heard it from the holy bishop himself. For the right reverend father was wont to suit his conversation to the age and ability of the hearers: and sometimes to bring in things he himself had done, that they might not lack hope of doing what they heard that he had been able to accomplish by the grace of God. So he related what I have formerly told you to boys: this story he cheerfully told to young men.

CHAPTER II

MEANWHILE the young Wulstan's father and mother had both grown weary of the world, and began to long and sigh earnestly for another habit and another way of life. Indeed old age and poverty lay before them. In no long time they satisfied their desire: and his father took the monk's habit at Worcester, his mother the nun's veil in the same city. The change of raiment called them to a better life: for it had been idle to put on other garments without growing in virtue. So with simple devotion and effectual desire they fulfilled their mind: and in due time departed this life. Wulstan continued for a time in the world, outwardly but not in heart, with his body not with his soul. Nevertheless, that by good example he might limn in himself the image of virtue, he entered the household of Brihtheah, Bishop of Worcester. The prelate gladly received him, both on the commendation of his kinsmen and of his own good will, seeing in him the grace of God and making it welcome. Wulstan, moreover, was no ill friend to himself, for he wrung favour even from hard and wicked men. All insolence, clamour, loose conduct, unmannerliness were far from him: he was never capricious or ill-tempered: and, what is a great adornment in the young, he most carefully guarded his modesty. The graces of his soul lost nothing by the beauty of his person. I may not count that among his virtues, but I cannot leave it out altogether; for, as the skill of the artificer is helped or hindered by what he works in, so virtue shines out more brightly in a comely body. By these qualities he did so win the love of the Bishop that of his own motion he advanced him to the priesthood though Wulstan could hardly be brought to consent. It is a notable thing in a young man that he counted himself unworthy of that office: not less notable that having received it he was a pattern of priesthood. He had not sought to attain it in self-confidence: when he had taken it upon him, he did not let it grow dull by slothfulness. By fasting and every kind of abstinence he took care to keep his body in subjection and give new strength to his soul. With his sobermindedness, his grave speech, his reverend bearing, his cheerful address he was already living the religious life in a secular habit. If he had occasion to rebuke any man, he so tempered his words that even when he was chiding he found something to praise. For that could not seem harsh which, though it sounded stern, savoured of love.

CHAPTER III

THE bishop more than once offered him a church near the city whereof the ample revenues would have been enough and more than enough to provide for his daily needs. Wulstan as often evaded the offer by putting off his answer from day to day: and at last, when the bishop pressed him hard, opened his mind to him. He said that the passing order of this world was losing its value for him: he desired to become a monk, and longed to offer to God not parts of his life, but the whole. At this answer the venerable bishop was filled with great joy; and roused the young man to livelier ardour by the trumpet call of his exhortation. Happy, he said, is the man who grows sick of the attractions of the world: the pleasure of them passes in a moment of time: the tooth of conscience gnaws as long as a man lives. Happy is the man who will become a monk: for as monks are utterly crucified to the world so are they most blessedly near to God. So they were of one mind, seeing that what the one desired the other pressed upon him. Wulstan became a monk at Worcester, and Brihtheah gave him his blessing and the monk's habit. Here if one desired to expatiate as an orator to his audience on all the blessings that happy day brought to Worcester which first saw Wulstan a monk, he would find his powers unequal to his purpose. What the tongue cannot utter let the mind strive to ponder. One thing must be said. Never in our days has there been a monk more free from faults, more perfect in virtues. Accordingly the brethren of that Church, finding his life blameless, soon made him schoolmaster, then precentor, and at last sacrist that he might have more abundant liberty for prayer, and richer opportunity of growing from virtue to virtue. Which occasion he most worthily embraced, and passed his days in fasting, and whole nights in watching. He counted among his joys what we slothful creatures account a great penance. Every day he genuflected at each verse of the seven psalms: and the same at night in the cxix psalm. In the western porch of the Church where there was an altar of All Saints with a banner of Our Lord, he would shut the door, and call upon Christ; assault heaven with his tears, and burden the air with lamentations. Feather bed or other bed he had none. He did not yield himself to sleep, but snatched it. He would lie with his head on the step before the altar, and his body on the bare ground. Or again he would put a book under his head and take a little sleep on bare boards. Before each of the eighteen altars that were in the Old Church he prostrated himself seven times a day. This he thought no hardship: what others thought a hardship he would copy. And while he stood high above others in virtue, he showed humility to everyman—and fulfilled without delay menial tasks from which others turned in disgust.

CHAPTER IV

IT became a habit with the blessed man to visit the churches of the neighbourhood by night, and say his office there; and in one after another to offer prayers to God. His way led through the midst of the cemetery, but his foot stumbled not, nor was his mind clouded by fear. Christ himself guided the soul of the righteous; that no darkness might trouble him, no loneliness make him tremble. The godly habit grew in him, nay, became as it were a second nature, so that soon he was going every night to the church of the Prince of the Apostles. This was formerly the bishop's seat: but Oswald had put out the secular canons, and well and wisely given the honour which had belonged to the Lord's apostle unto the Mother of the Lord. So Wulstan stood praying before the altar, his whole being yearning to God. Then the old enemy, who never fails to grudge us good or to suggest evil, putting on the form of a certain countryman, thus broke in upon his prayers. What madness, he asked, hath brought thee hither in the horrid darkness of the night? Thy coming is ill-timed, and pleaseth me not. Then he challenged him to combat, that he might put to the proof the bodily strength of one whose spirit was so daring. This with hideous grin and furious voice. But Wulstan little moved, for he fully perceived that the Enemy was hidden in that disguise, went on reciting his psalms: and by chance, or rather by God's providence he was repeating the verse *The Lord is my helper: I will not fear what man can do unto me.* Even as he spake the enemy fell on him, winding his sinewy arms about the saint's body wasted with fasting. He first thrust back the monster, then attacked in his turn. Nay, finding that the Devil was lurking behind that mask, he took courage for the fight, wielding the arms of faith. The struggle went on through no small part of the night, the impudence of the Devil matched against the confidence of a saint. It was a cruel and wicked thing—that a spirit should wrestle with a man, not with the purpose of putting his powers to the proof, but in sheer hatred of the power he had proved. But Wulstan's ready and noble courage yielded not to that fury which, as we know, God sometimes suffers to trouble the earth and the sea. Wherefore at last the grisly shade giving way before Wulstan's valiant faith, and vexing the air around with a foul stench, melted away and vanished. But, lest he should seem to have achieved nothing, he trampled with all the weight of wickedness on the good man's foot, and thrust it through as it were with a hot iron. The poison came even into his bones, as Godric a monk of that same convent bears witness: who, as Coleman relates, said he had often seen that wound or sore: I know not which to call it. Coleman also declares that he knew the countryman whose semblance the enemy had put on. And surely he was the right man, with his monstrous strength, his foul crimes, and his hideous face, for the wickedest robber of all to change into—that robber from whom proceed all things unclean and abominable that the world has seen or shall see hereafter.

CHAPTER V

AS time went on the seed of every virtue grew and flourished in Wulstan—and above all the virtue of obedience and submission to them who were set over him. Every hard, every painful task that was set him found in him the will if not peradventure the power to do it. For this cause and by divine grace all men loved him dearly, so that they accounted worthy of all observance one whom the mercy of heaven held accepted. Most of all the Bishop was so affected towards Wulstan that he thought him worthy of any honour. The diligent performance of the offices he had held filled him with hope that he would prove worthy of higher dignity if it were conferred upon him. So, when he came to be appointed Provost, or as it is now called Prior, of the monks, he grasped the opportunity of showing his quality, and reformed many things that were amiss both within the House and without. The revenues of the Priory which had gone to ruin by the carelessness of his predecessors he vigorously restored to a firm footing: and within he enforced observance of the Rule. And to do this more effectually he gave the godly example of his own life to the brethren under him: being ashamed to preach what he was not ready to perform. What he preached was not of his own devising put forth with fairseeming words. He diligently studied the writings of the fathers and what he thirstily drank from the founts of doctrine, that he poured forth in honeyed streams. For so I may borrow a saying from the life of S. Gregory: a saying which Coleman has turned into English with much else, and I have put back again into Latin. And as he spent long hours in study of all the books of Holy Scripture, so did he give heed especially to those which commend chastity, a virtue which he followed earnestly in himself, and sharply rebuked the lack of in others; as will now appear.

CHAPTER VI

THERE was in the same city a wife, whose house was well provided above what is needful for life, and whose comely person was apt to draw the curious eyes of them that looked on it. She came often to the Church, but rather to be gazed at than to hearken to the oracles of God, as was proved by her daring to court the Prior with words of flattery. It was vain, for

Wulstan's modesty was far above her beauty and her promises. For a while she nursed her hidden wound, and was afraid to show it; but at last her desire grew stronger than her shame, and as the Prior chanced to be standing near her in the Church, she took hold of his garment. He checked her with a stern glance—but she begged him in God's name not to reject what she had to say. Wulstan supposing she wished to make her confession went aside with her. But the woman, seizing her opportunity, began to whisper in the holy man's ears words of evil counsel savouring of the wiles of woman and the cunning of the serpent. For a long time she had thought of speaking to him of a thing which might well be of profit to them both. She had a home abounding in riches, but with no man to govern it. Both her parents were dead, and her husband far away. Wulstan's wisdom should take upon it the charge. He should rule the household at his will: and order the spending of the money. On that he bade her give her money to the poor, and herself take the veil: but she replied, not so: what she desired and implored was that he should lay aside for a moment his priestly strictness and consent to share her bed. 'Twas but a little fault to enjoy the embraces of a woman: even if it were a somewhat grave fault he could redeem the guilt of a venial sin by almsgiving from her wealth. She had enough and to spare, and she would not grudge it. The Prior endured no more: but breaking in upon her speech, and making the sign of the Cross on his forehead, Away, he cried, with the hatred thou dost deserve, thou fuel of lust, thou vessel of Satan. His stern words were followed by a blow with his open hand, which, in his zeal for chastity he laid so heartily on the cheek of the snarling woman that the sound of it was heard outside the doors of the church.

The story of this deed ran through the town, and was for many days spoken of wherever men met together—how this second Joseph rejected a wanton woman in his heart, and smote her with his hand.

CHAPTER VII

NOR was it only upon the monks, but upon the common people also that Wulstan scattered the seed of his loving kindness. For often in the morning, when the day's duties were done, he was to be seen standing before the doors of the Church that those who would speak with him might have easier access. Never weary in well-doing he would often prolong his day there till noon, and even till evensong, if he could help those who had suffered violence, or baptize the children of the poor. For already the love of money had crept up from the shades below, so that priests refused to administer that sacrament to infants unless the parents would fill their pockets. So Wulstan, pitying the destitution of the parents, pitying also the avarice of the priests in his heart while he scourged it by his act, busied himself with a task of exceeding lovingkindness in baptizing poor children. The people ran to him from the towns and the fields—especially those who could not well give money to buy for their children the laver of baptism. The custom spread from the poor to the rich—and soon no one in that region thought a child duly baptized unless Wulstan had baptized it—and they were confirmed in their doubts by what they rightly judged concerning Wulstan's holiness and devotion. His fame went abroad through England—so that the greatest nobles of the land eagerly sought his friendship, and held it fast. They looked to it as a safeguard in prosperity, a refuge in adversity, and a protection in all changes of fortune. Among them Harold, feeling himself capable of greater powers, and already claiming the kingdom by his noble qualities, loved Wulstan above all men. When he was on a journey he counted it nothing to turn aside thirty miles that in converse with Wulstan he might forget the burden of his cares. So wholly was he given to his will and guidance, that Wulstan might be ashamed to command, but it never irked Harold to obey. No less dearly did the Saint love the Earl. He received his confession kindly, and was the faithful interpreter of his prayers to God. In the same path of good-will did walk, Aldred the Bishop of Worcester after Brihtheah, a man subtle in the affairs of the world, yet not without religion. He did greatly observe the Lord Prior for his holiness and humbly obey him; and in all things bowed to him as to a very dear father.

CHAPTER VIII

THERE is another matter which I will not withhold from my readers: for it deserves a chapter as well as anything that I have told. Wulstan perceived that the people were falling away for lack of preaching: so on every Sunday and on all great festivals he poured into their ears the counsels of salvation. You would have thought the words which he spake to the people from his high place sounded from the treasure of the evangelists and prophets so did he thunder against sinners, and pour refreshing rain on the elect. This he did with perfect modesty, and in his humility would not have had it noised abroad. Yet for all his humility envy found him out and pricked at him. There was in that same church a monk from over sea, Winrich, by name, well furnished with learning, a vigorous and ready speaker, wise after the wisdom of this world, of polished manners; and accordingly acceptable and well seen of men. He was on the other hand hot tempered, and prone to attack with bitter envy what did not please him. So he had much fault to find with the Saint's preaching; and spake in this manner. It was irregular, because he was assuming the Bishop's office. To the Bishop alone it belonged to preach: because he alone by the power committed to him could absolve the people from their sins. For a monk the silence of the cloister was enough: it was not for him to insult people's ears with stately gesture and speech. It looked more like a crafty striving after preferment than the discharge of a pious duty. Such things he said, not only behind Wulstan's back, but one day in a fit of temper straight to his face. He, armed with the shield of patience, answered but little. There could be nothing more pleasing to God than to recall to the way of truth the people who were straying into sin. If Winrich could show him anything more pleasing to Christ he would straightway do it. So they parted, and went to rest. But God, to show how highly He accounted of what Wulstan had done, smote the slanderer with a frightful vision. When he had laid himself down to sleep upon his bed, he seemed to be carried before the judgment seat of an unknown judge, who wrathfully demanded of him why he had that day reviled his servant for the good deed of preaching—and as he murmured excuses, it was commanded that he should be cast down on the pavement and beaten. Thereon the officers drew near and beat him sore, and he could only cry in torment, Have mercy, Lord, Lord have mercy. At last he was loosed, and was asked whether he would any more forbid the Lord's herald. In that dreadful moment he was ready to swear by all that was holy not only that he would not forbid, but that he would urge Wulstan and others to preach, if only the mercy of the judge would suffer him to live and escape the anguish of that hour. So, having pledged himself not to break his promise, he was sent away. Accordingly, as soon as he could, and that was as soon as day dawned, he fell at Wulstan's feet and embraced his knees. He confessed his fault and begged for pardon. When he was asked what had wrought the sudden change of mind, he told the story of his dream, swearing that it was true. His streaming tears and unfeigned prayers were surety of its truth: and the black and swollen bruises on his shoulders bore witness that the vision was real; it was no light chastisement that he had suffered. The saint readily forgave him, and at his blessing Winrich was healed and the pain went out of him. This miracle which happened in our own day may well win belief, and may free from all doubt the ancient tradition that a like chastisement befell blessed Hierome. For it makes little difference that he was beaten for reading in heathen authors, and Winrich for forbidding to preach. It is almost the same sin to neglect holy scripture for the idle writings of heathen men, and to will that the scripture be not preached.

About this same time Wulstan was designing a building above the roof of the Church for bells to hang in. What is the right name for such a structure I cannot at the moment recall. For this purpose he provided step-ladders for the workmen to stand on, and make firm the steps still hanging in the air. And now ladder above ladder stood fastened with cords reaching almost to the sky, whereby the builders were bidden to carry out the work. One bolder workman, fain to climb higher than his fellows on the sheer ascent, fell headlong. Wulstan was standing by; and while the man was tumbling down that height of air, set the Cross between him and destruction. Thou, O Christ, wert there to save: Thou wert There to pity, and to set Thine hand under him, O King of pity. The man fell not less than forty feet—but not only was his body not broken, but his mind was not stunned as is wont to happen when the blood runs cold. He arose unhurt, blaming his own rashness that he had fallen, and blessing Wulstan's holiness that he had come off without harm. If Wulstan had not been there the workman would have lost not one but, as the saying is, a hundred lives. I might have set forth this miracle at greater length—but it were impertinent to multiply words when the thing itself exacts wonder and admiration.

CHAPTER IX

MEANWHILE King Edward sent Bishop Aldred to the Emperor Henry at Cologne to set in order some matters, which do not concern us. Aldred found favour in the eyes of the Imperial Majesty, and abode there some days to rest after his labours. And either for his own sake or because he was the Ambassador of so great a king, he received many gifts: and a certain man gave him as a parting gift the psalter and sacramentary of which I spoke before. Cnut had formerly sent both these books to Cologne that the people there might remember him kindly. Aldred, knowing nothing of Wulstan's prophetic saying, when he came home, gave them back to Wulstan accounting him the only man whose life was worthy of such books. He received them as a gift from heaven, greatly rejoicing and giving thanks to God for the fulfilment of his godly desire.

CHAPTER X

IN the year that Cynesige Archbishop of York ended his days Aldred of Worcester was acclaimed his successor. The thing pleased Edward the simple-hearted king. Aldred, as the custom is, went his way to Rome, but found Pope Nicholas at first no friend to his desires: for Aldred was not minded to give up Worcester, and the Pope would not grant him the pallium for York unless he resigned Worcester. Aldred was so bound by ties of love to Worcester that it was dearer to him than the dignity of the Archbishopric. So, after long disputation, Aldred turned homeward and came to Sutri, Earl Tostig who was with him breathing threatenings that for this there should be no more paying of Peter's Pence from England. However, they were attacked by robbers and stripped, to the great scrrow of beholders, and made their way back to Rome. Their sufferings so far melted the rigour of the Apostolic See that Aldred received the pallium of York, having pledged himself to resign Worcester provided that he could find a better priest in the diocese to put in his place. As witnesses to his promise, and to settle other ecclesiastical matters in England certain cardinals were sent with him, whom he presented to the king. The godly prince received them as his excellent custom was, conforming in all things to the ways of the Roman Church. He entertained them with great honour and reverence for a time, and committed them to Aldred to bring them on their journeys, and send them back to the Court for Easter. For the Cardinals would know Aldred well seeing he had companied with them so long, and could converse with him freely and live with him as with a familiar friend. According to the tenor of the apostolic precept Aldred travelled with them almost all over England, and came again to Worcester a little before Lent. From there he went to visit his estates; and lodged them with Wulstan the Prior. They were glad enough to be at ease and take rest after the toils of their journeyings. Moreover, the kindness of Wulstan left nothing undone that they might know by experience how free and bounteous is the hospitality of the English. Himself meanwhile forgot not to be as was his wont instant in prayer and fasting. Whole nights he spent in watching and saying of psalms: often bowing his knees: altogether scorning sleep. Thrice in the week he abstained altogether from food, and continued his fast through the night until dawn. On those days, that he might not offend in word, he bridled his tongue with unbroken silence. On the other three days of the week his food was leeks and boiled cabbage with a crust of bread. On Sundays, in honour of the feast, he mended his spare diet with fish and wine—but rather to control his natural appetite than to pamper his belly—Every day he lovingly entertained three poor men, and following the Lord's command, gave them their daily bread and washed their feet.

CHAPTER XI

THUS were the hearts of the Cardinals moved to admire his life and praise his teaching which commanded the more respect in that he first practised what he preached. Thus, when they had returned to the Court, and the choice of a Bishop of Worcester was spoken of, they put forward Wulstan's name. He, they said, was worthy of a bishopric who had added more honour to the priestly office than he had received from it: whose nature answered to his diligence: in whom life squared with wisdom. For this surely is wisdom: to live well: to make deeds prevent words. By these praises they aroused the goodwill of King Edward in whom the trafficker in benefices and the covetous man never found anything to forward their designs. The Archbishops of Canterbury and York gave their support to the Cardinals, the one of kindness, the other of knowledge: both by their sentence. With them in praising Wulstan were the Earls Harold and Elfgar, men more famed for warlike courage than for religion. They bestirred themselves vigorously in his cause, sending mounted messengers on Wulstans' behalf, who rode many miles in little time to hasten on the matter. So the Saint was presented to the Court, and bidden to take upon him the office of Bishop. He earnestly withstood them, crying out that he was unequal to so great a charge, while all men cried that he was equal to it. So entirely was the whole people agreed, that it were not wrong to say that in all those bodies there was, concerning this matter. but one mind. But, to be brief, the cardinals and archbishops would have lost their labour, had they not pleaded against his unwillingness the duty of obeying the Pope. To that plea he must needs yield, and assented to the election, worthy, unwilling, compelled. Notably and rightly the resistance of one man gave way to the will of God and the people. I may say solemnly that his advancement was the will of God—for he never did of purpose anything against God's will—and casual faults he washed away by fruitful penance.

I must not forget to say that there was at that time Abbot of Evesham a man named Ethelwig, full of worldly wisdom, and by no means lacking in religion. Aldred, remembering his promise to the Pope, had hesitated for a while whether to choose for the bishopric Ethelwig the man of the world, or Wulstan the Saint. For these two men stood out above their fellows in the Diocese of Worcester in this way and in that. However when he had fully weighed their claims, though Ethelwig pressed his suit heavily, man's prudence gave way to divine providence.

CHAPTER XII

SO King Edward well and truly invested Wulstan with the Bishopric of Worcester—though Aldred had influence enough to rob him, as will appear later, of nearly all of its estates. The holy man did not suffer this gladly: but hid his griefs in silence, counting it wiser to yield to circumstances. Not long after he was consecrated at York by that same Archbishop: because

Stigand of Canterbury was under the Pope's interdict. The reason of this interdict it is not convenient to explain here. Those who wish to know it can read it in my other writings. One may well believe that God meant it to be said prophetically of Wulstan, *Behold an Israelite indeed in whom is no guile*. Nothing can appear more true for any man who has seen, heard, or read of his life. So little did he desire to have the office of Bishop laid upon him, that he declared, as those who were present testify, that he would rather have lost his head than have had it happen to him. He was even ready to fly to some distant place, but his friends took care to hinder him. They cheered his downcast soul, some by words of persuasion, some by words of counsel. They pleaded with him, falling at his knees and feet and often kissing them. They warned him not to spoil the free gift of heaven by impatience, but to adorn it by bearing it meekly. Obedience, they said, was the seal of all virtues—the man who would not obey could not be accounted either a faithful monk to his cloister or a faithful bishop to his flock. So he must not only bear it humbly, but thank God who had raised him to an office which should be a blessing to those over whom he should bear rule. So spake they—But it cannot be doubted that in the saint's breast there was a dreadful conflict between two opposing powers, Love and Fear: Fear, lest he should fail under a burden to which he was not accustomed: and Love, forbidding him to strive against the commanding authority of so many worthy men, and the earnest devotion of the people; for the more unworthy he thought himself the more eagerly did they press it on him; and he gave them the more reason to believe he would discharge it wisely by coming to it with such anxious searchings of heart. For it is a fool's part to plunge heedlessly into a business without knowing how much labour it will need to perform it.

CHAPTER XIII

WHEN he had been consecrated, as I was saying, Aldred left him at York professing thereby to do him honour: and for no little while Worcester mourned his absence. Meanwhile the Archbishop diverted the revenues of that church to his own uses. Hardly, when at last Wulstan returned, did he give him seven villages, and stubbornly retained all the rest. Wulstan knew nothing could be done with him by force: but he so wrought upon the avarice of that proud soul by his prayers, that he restored all but twelve villages to the Church of Worcester. When and how our good father recovered the twelve my pen shall relate anon.

CHAPTER XIV

TO return to my story. Wulstan being raised to be a bishop straightway turned his mind to works of piety. Straightway indeed: for on the morrow of his consecration he dedicated a church to blessed Bede. Rightly did he begin by dedicating a Church to him whose name stands first in English letters. That day he watered the people with so flowing a discourse that none might doubt that Wulstan was inspired by the Holy Spirit with the same eloquence that of old had moved the tongue of Bede. And not only then but all his life the fame of his preaching did so move the people that you might see them assemble in multitudes wheresoever they heard that he was to dedicate a Church. He himself gladly sought occasion of preaching—and ever spake Christ, ever set Christ before his hearers: Nay, so to say it, he dragged Christ unto him though He would not: for so stubbornly did he continue in watchings and fastings, such violent prayers did he cast up to heaven, that of him and men like him justly hath the Lord said, *The Kingdom of heaven suffereth violence, and the violent take it by force.* So level did he keep the balance of his life, that he held fast to either calling, and loosed his hold on neither. A Bishop, he was still true to the religious rule of a monk. A monk, he showed the authority of a Bishop. Far removed was he in all his ways from the men our age can show. If one came to consult him, he was full of counsel—if one came to him with a request he was right easy of access. If something was to be granted or refused, he was impartial in considering, swift in deciding. When he had to judge, he leaned to the side of mercy. He did not ply the rich for gifts, nor reject the poor for his poverty. He never yielded to flattery, nor loved a flatterer. Never did he depart from justice for the fear of great men, nor pay them any honour they had not deserved. When he was praised for a good deed, he praised the grace of God for it and was not proud. When he was reviled, he forgave those who reviled him, secure in a good conscience. But that was not often: because, as he cherished every man in love as a son, so all in return loved him as a father. With merry heart and cheerful countenance he was already tasting in hope the waters of the fountain of heavenly gladness: whereof now indeed he is drinking long draughts. His soul was always busy with inward things—yet men did not find him slack or lazy with outward things. He built many churches about the diocese, beginning them with zeal and completing them nobly. Chief of them was the Cathedral Church which he erected from the foundation to the last stone. The number of the monks in it was increased and brought under the Rule of the Order. But this and other things that Wulstan did are always before your eyes, and may be briefly set down. Wherefore, that my discourse may turn to a wider field, let me tell the rest of my story as quickly as I may.

CHAPTER XV

HE adorned the office of a Bishop in many ways, and especially in this that he visited his diocese diligently—gave baptism to any children that were yet unbaptized, and exhorted the people to faith and good works. When he came to a chapel, no haste or press of business could make him pass in without a salutation. Rather would he enter in and offer the incense of his prayers, and of the tears which one saith were always at his command, to God and the Saint whose shrine it was. Thus on a day when he had been called to the Shire Court and was passing through

Evesham, his clerks begged him not to turn aside to the Church: but he would not heed them. So he went in and fell down before the relics of S. Egwin and prayed earnestly for himself and his people. When he had made his prayer he saluted all the monks with a kiss, and comforted them with a goodly discourse. There was in the monastery a certain monk who had long been sick of a fever and lay dying, as they supposed, upon his bed. He, hearing that the Bishop was in the house sent a messenger to tell him how he wept and earnestly desired to look upon his face before he breathed his last. The Bishop when he heard it did not put him off with excuses; and when his company pleaded that it would delay their journey and that the day was passing, he answered, My work is to fulfil the command of my Master to visit the sick. And if you hinder me from fulfilling it, and this man depart hence, I shall be guilty of evading the commandment. Even as he spake he went in to the sick man and eased his pain with consoling promises, that he would hear his confession while he lived, and give him the last rites when dying. The monk, who desired nothing less than to depart this life without confession and absolution, appealed to the pity of the Bishop to obtain for him this benefit: and his hopeless distress touched the heart of Wulstan. His bowels melted with pity for the poor man: and lifting heart and hands to God, he prayed: Almighty and merciful God of whose gift it cometh that repentance washeth away sins: in whose sight he that accuseth himself is absolved: I humbly beseech thee that thou wilt vouchsafe to grant life to this sick man till thou mayest receive his soul cleansed by penitence. He spake, and added to his prayer a blessing. Prayer and blessing alike ascended to heaven, and the goodness of God tarried not in granting the petition of His faithful servant. Even as the Bishop went forth there went forth also the pains of the sufferer: all his weakness fled, and strength and health abounded to drive out the disease. Straightway he was fain to arise, and called for his raiment and his shoes, rejecting the bed whereon he had lain so long. His brethren thought he spake with wandering mind, as does befall when the brain is disordered and the seat of reason troubled, and sick men utter words at random. But Eigelric, for that was the monk's name, ceased not to bless God and the Bishop for his healing; and left his bed whole and hearty, and bade the rest do as he did in praising God and Wulstan.

CHAPTER XVI

IN the fifth year of Wulstan's bishopric King Edward departing this life left a seed-bed of grievous strife to England: for both Harold and William Count of Normandy laid claim to it as of right. Harold, whether it was by goodwill or by force that he gained it, became master of almost the whole kingdom. Only the Northumbrians, a great and turbulent folk, were not ready to submit. They vowed that they would not suffer the proud North to yield to the feeble South. Their lust for power and their fierce temper were inflamed by Tostig, the king's own brother, a man of un-

d

failing courage if he had but chosen to turn his hot spirit to the pursuits of peace. Thereafter he was slain in that same land together with Harold king of Norway, whom he had brought in to his aid; and so paid the price of his rash daring. But this was not yet. At that time Harold being about to depart thither, that he might bring down their pride by gentler remedies not being minded to break it with the sword, called Wulstan to him. For the fame of his holiness had so found a way to the remotest tribes, that it was believed that he could quell the most stubborn insolence. And so it came to pass. For those tribes, untameable by the sword, and haughty from generation to generation, yet for the reverence they bore to the Bishop, easily yielded allegiance to Harold. And they would have continued in that way, had not Tostig, as I have said, turned them aside from it. Wulstan, good, gentle, and kindly though he was, spake not smooth things to the sinners, but rebuked their vices, and threatened them with evil to come. If they were still rebellious, he warned them plainly, they should pay the penalty in suffering. Never did his human wisdom or his gift of prophecy deceive him. Many things to come, both on that journey and at other times, did he foretell. Moreover he spake plainly to Harold of the calamities which should befall him and all England if he should not bethink himself to correct their wicked ways. For in those days the English were for the most part very evil livers; and in peace and the abundance of pleasant things luxury flourished. Wulstan was the enemy of all vice, and especially abhorred the fashion of growing the hair long. If any man would yield him his head, he himself cut away the wanton locks. For this purpose he kept a little knife with which he used to cut his nails and scrape blots from books. Having thus taken as it were the first fruits, he enjoined them by their obedience to shorten the rest of the hair to match what he had done. If any man thought fit to refuse he would frankly blame his softness and threaten him with evil to come. It should come to pass, he said, that men who were ashamed to be men, and made themselves like women with flowing tresses, should be no better than women in defence of their country against men from oversea. Which manifestly appeared at the coming of the Normans that same year: who can deny it? And now that we are come to the time of the Normans this First Book may draw to an end. For I think it will be more convenient to relate severally what this most holy man did in the time of the English, and what he did in the time of the Normans, just as Coleman ended his first book with Wulstan's election to the Bishopric. Moreover, I will not hide from you, reverend brethren, that I have left out nearly all the names of witnesses that I might not wound the delicate ears of the readers by their barbarous sound. Also I have left out some fine words and phrases which Coleman borrowed from the Acts of other saints, and in his blind devotion inserted. For, as I have said already, when the truth is high enough, the man who tries to raise it with fine words loses his labour. When he is trying to praise he dishonours and diminishes: for it seems as if he cannot trust his own story, but must needs borrow help from another.

Here ends the First Book.

Here begins the Second Book.

CHAPTER I

MEANWHILE William Count of Normandy came to England and met Harold in battle, and slew him and smote the English with a great slaughter and took the kingdom to himself. Then was Wulstan's prophecy fulfilled: for the wretched people of the land were so feeble and foolish that after the first encounter they were never at one in striving to win back their freedom, as if all the whole strength of England had fallen with Harold. King William did naught to vex our holy man. Nay rather he did greatly honour him; and loved him and spake to him as his father. Wulstan therefore, taking the opportunity, restored to their proper use many possessions of the Church of Worcester which the insolence of the Danes or the power of Aldred the Archbishop had stripped from it. With such favour did the king look upon him. So doth holiness win the love of the great ones of the world: so is true religion revered by men whom others much fear.

Thomas, a Canon of Bayeux, came to York in Aldred's place: he was a man of notable learning; not unversed in business: one that might be accounted better in life and conversation than his fellows, and of a surety, first of all in music. Against him Wulstan, the man of God, brought a plea concerning those villages of the church which Aldred, as we have said, had seized and never given back, and Wulstan was claiming as lawfully his own. Thomas on the other hand not only held that the estates should not be restored, but, not being an Englishman, and hearkening to whisperers, went on to declare that the Church of Worcester belonged to him. The rule over it, he said, came to him by lawful succession: the Archbishop of York had held it before him. He pressed his cause with great vigour, first in England, and later in the presence of Lanfranc before Pope Alexander. Lanfranc was sore troubled, for he saw that the rights of his Church were in danger if he held his peace: but in his answer he was more moved by justice than by wrath. Then the Pope, loth to offend Lanfranc who in former days had been his master, yet not willing to press hard upon Thomas, to rid himself of an ungracious decision committed the matter to an English Council. So the case was fought out before an assembly of the nobles of England. Thomas had for his helper Odo, who in riches rivalled the King to whom he was nearly allied in blood. For this Odo, Earl of Kent and Bishop of Bayeux, was William's half-brother. With him came a host of great men, some won by gifts, some by flattery. Lanfranc alone stood on the side of justice. For the king too, inclined to favour his brother though Lanfranc was of some weight in his reckoning. Well—the parties were set and the cause was opened. Thomas went out with his friends to make ready his plea and his answer to them that were against him. Wulstan meanwhile laid him down and slept peacefully. Thomas came in again and spake with ready wit, and a great flood of words. Wulstan, awoken by his friends, had psalms on his lips, prayers in his heart. At last he was bidden to go out and take thought how he might make his answer bright and sharp. Forth he went, with little following, and straightway began the Office of None and sang it to the end. And when his friends told him that he had better be thinking of other things than psalms, and be about his business, he replied: Ye fools, know ye not what Our Lord said—*When ye shall stand before Kings and Governors take no thought how or what ye shall speak. For it shall be given you in that hour what ye shall speak.* Himself my creator the Lord Jesus Christ who spake this is able to give me to-day words wherewith to defend the righteousness of my cause, and bring down the crooked counsels of them. It was a glorious saying. He had then in his hands the lives of the blessed prelates Dunstan and Oswald, who both in their days had been set over Worcester, whose lives he copied, whose wisdom he observed. And with the wondrous clearness of the eyes of faith he professed that he beheld them there before him and doubted not that they were come as his advocates. He returned to the hall, and without trouble won his cause. When the king asked him what he had found in his counsel, he answered, 'my counsel is in you.' Straightway William, since *the king's heart is in the hand of God*, put forth a decree, as Lanfranc urged, that the Bishop of Worcester should be subject to Canterbury, and the Archbishop of York had no rights over him. Moreover he granted to the Church of Worcester the twelve villages which Aldred had held for his own profit till the day of his death: and of his royal bounty recompensed the Archbishop with other estates. Yet more marvellous is it that at that same Council which was held by the river Parret Archbishop Lanfranc committed to Wulstan the visitation of the Diocese of Chester. That part of England, which has three Shires, Chester, Salop and Stafford, was so far off that the Normans had not yet come to it, and on account of its barbarity unsubdued. This commission was much spoken of, and all men marvelled at the abundance of the grace of God bestowed upon Wulstan. For he departed from the Council bearing two bishoprics who had come there in peril of losing one. As witness of this story, Coleman cited Walkelin, Bishop of Winchester who stood next to Lanfranc at that time in good qualities, but far behind him. More than once he had heard that Bishop tell how the holy man, matched almost single against so many men of great place and keen understanding, had come off victorious.

CHAPTER II

SO much for that. Now that I may tell of some of the mighty works which Christ wrought by Wulstan, let me spread my sails to the wind of Heaven and push forth into the deep. Of his gift of prophecy there are many proofs—it will be enough to touch on two. One Aldwin, a professed monk, but unlettered, had attempted to found a religious house at Malvern; but after some years he was discouraged by the greatness of the task, and was minded to give it up. But, because it would be rash to depart without the knowledge of the Bishop, he went to him and set before the holy man his difficulties and his lack of money. He was fain, he said, to make a pilgrimage to Jerusalem, that, if he could not bring in others, he might dedicate himself to the service of God. Nay, quoth the Bishop, Believe me (for that was the strongest oath he used), if thou knewest what a great House God foreseeth in that place, thou wouldest rejoice exceedingly. Aldwin believed the word of prophecy, and persevered—and proved the truth thereof in the sweat of his brow as today may be seen.

CHAPTER III

THAT which follows is like unto the former. Wulstan had occasion, as I have said, to visit the diocese of Chester—and often passing through Shrewsbury, he was wont to spend nights watching with prayer in the Chapel of S. Peter, then the least in the City. The townsmen wondered and curiously enquired of him why he passed by the Church called S. Mary's, and honoured that chapel with his prayers. It is known that the Bishop answered, Believe me, this chapel which you despise shall be hereafter the most glorious place in all Shrewsbury, and the joy of the whole province—and ye shall love it while ye live and lie in it when ye die. So he spake at that time, and the thing came to pass according to his promise, as is too well known to you for me to ply my pen in telling you of it.

CHAPTER IV

THE divine acceptance of his virtues bestowed on Wulstan this grace: that after the manner of the ancient fathers he should excel in driving away diseases. He who strove to equal the pattern of their lives, might justly receive the glorious sign of working miracles. A few of them which have not escaped my memory I will briefly record. And, as I spake before of the monk healed at Evesham, so now I will tell in very few words about the good work wrought upon a woman in the same place. There was a woman dwelling thereabout, in a well-plenished home: but an evil spirit had robbed her of her wits. At first it made her an idiot, then drove her to violent frenzy. And now she had come to that state of misery that she fled from the love of her parents and the care of her kindred, and wandered through desolate places or wherever the impulse of madness carried her. Her parents, who had been vexed before, thought this was not to be borne. They laid hands on her and bound her with fetters. Too harsh, one might say. But in truth their harshness was followed by pity, and the more wretched she became the more earnestly did they hunt for remedies. They hired physicians to heal the distemper by the art of physic. They brought priests to recall her mind by healing exorcism. Among them came the Prior of Evesham, who told and testified the truth of it to Coleman: but he, like the others, went away disappointed. For although physicians and clerks did their utmost, they wasted their medicines and their exorcisms. And indeed her kinsfolk spent most of their substance: and were left without hope or counsel. So they went back to the said prior for they knew he was a good man, and asked him what they should do. If he knew of any hope yet remaining, let him tell them: and they would assuredly do it if it were not beyond their power. He thought it over and advised them to show her to Bishop Wulstan. He and they ought to have faith: for no sickness dared exist before him who rejoiced to submit himself to the commands of the Creator. The thing seemed good to them, and they went to the Bishop: and easily obtained what they desired. For as soon as he beheld the woman he was grieved to the heart by her sufferings: her fearful calamity drew a groan from him: groaning he found a remedy. He stretched forth his hand and gave the woman his blessing. Straightway, in a moment, the sick woman recovered her senses and was of sound mind: she knew her kinsmen: she blessed the Bishop. He followed up the heavenly gift with words of wholesome counsel: Go in peace: Bless not Wulstan, but God: love virtue: sin no more: keep innocency: lest a worse thing come unto thee. The seed of preaching could not but bear fruit when it was sown by so expert a husbandman. The woman soon put on the veil of a nun, and set the precepts of God above the World.

CHAPTER V

WULSTAN showed like power over a like distemper at a village called Cleeve in Gloucestershire. There dwelt a husbandman who earned a good living by the labour of his hands. Him so evil a spirit had possessed that he tore in pieces with his hands or gnawed with his teeth everything he could reach; at what was beyond his reach he would grind his teeth, cursing and spitting. The villagers must needs come together, if peradventure they might find a remedy for the mischief; his kinsmen and neighbours especially pitying his misery. So despite his struggles they bound him with raw hides: but he seized the thongs in his teeth and bit them through or burst them like threads of tow. Then they bethought them of fetters that might avail against his violence, and bound him, crying aloud, with chains of iron, and made him fast to a bedpost. So held he uttered frightful bellowings rather than cries, so that the mad noise brought fear even on those who were afar off. It was as if a legion were speaking from the mouth of one with a multitude of confused voices. The Bishop was sojourning in that same village which was his own: and the man's kindred carried their trouble to him. They implored him to come to the wretch, seeing that he was a burden too great to be brought to the Bishop. He tarried not, but sighing deeply, followed them to the house. The sufferer, as soon as he beheld Wulstan, began to tremble in all his limbs and roar aloud: he grinned and reviled the saint, and cast spittle at him from his gaping jaws. His sad estate grieved the heart of the good bishop: and spreading his hands to heaven he prayed: Lord Jesus Christ, who by thy death hast delivered the race of man from the power of the Devil; who didst suffer the Legion cast out from a man to go into the swine: deliver this man from the devil, and give him back his right mind. Then, turning to the evil spirit: Depart, foul spirit from this image of God, and give honour to the Holy Spirit. Wondrous to tell, wondrous to believe what followed. The man who had been mad put off his frenzy, and ceasing to roll his bloodshot eyes came to his wits again. He mended from hour to hour, and when the bishop returned to his own place, he was wholly free from madness. This man lived for many years, and after the blessed man's death testified to his miracles, a witness more worthy of trust in as much as he himself had that blessed experience of his power.

CHAPTER VI

NOT many days after, Wulstan's steward sent him a messenger on some business of the household. This man was what they call a squire: and an ill-starred journey it was for him. When he had gone a little way a spirit of unrest seized him, and troubled him sorely by the judgment of God which is sometimes hidden, never unjust. He lost his wits, and eschewing the company of men fled into a wood hard by, and abode there night and day. The country folk were vexed by such unseemly doings, and caught him and bound him fast with cords. But anon he had a careless watcher, and ridding himself of his bonds sought the grove again. The people were so affrighted that they dared not go near the place where they knew he was, either because he had done some hurt to one of them, or because it is natural to look with horror on a man who has lost the semblance of man. Meanwhile the Bishop came as the evening was passing into night, for he had travelled somewhat later than daylight lasted. He was even now going to rest when the news came of the man's misfortune, and all his servants were crying out about it. Straightway God's priest enjoined on them their religious duty; and bade them pray for the sufferer and say the Lord's Prayer. It was his custom when in any place at any hour he heard of a man's death or grievous sickness, to bid his people pray that the dead might rest in peace, or the sick be healed of his infirmity. Marvellous is the clemency of Christ: memorable the grace given to Wulstan. That same night the young wanderer's mind grew clear. He returned unbidden to the village, and mingled with his fellow-servants: and never thereafter showed the least sign of madness.

CHAPTER VII

THERE is a village of the bishopric called Kempsey whereat the Bishop was sojourning in its season. Thither had come a poor man from Kent, who sat with others daily to receive alms. Not only was he poor, but stricken with a sore disease which they call the King's evil. It had gradually so poisoned all his members that you could not rightly say he had a body, but went about with a living corpse. He was horrible to behold, for he was all running with foul matter: horrible to hear, for his speech was a kind of hoarse whining. At the last Arthur, the bishop's steward, who is witness for this and other matters concerning Wulstan, was implored by him to hear what he had to say. Once and again Arthur shrank from him: but at length, constrained by his adjuring him in the name of God, stayed and bade him say on. The poor man mumbling and panting, and hard to be understood, told him that he came from Kent, and was full of a vile disease, as Arthur could see. Thrice he had been bidden in a dream to present himself to the Bishop in hope of being healed; and therefore had he come. He begged Arthur to tell his lord, and plead with him in the name of God. The servant carried the message; but Wulstan who shrank from the praise of men, did not hear him gladly. Nay, it is not for me, he said, to essay any miracle, much less a miracle so great as this—go and give the sick man food and clothing, that he may at least have the consolation of thus much charity to repay him for his weary journey. So his counsel would have come to naught, but that Elmer the priest began to be anxious and troubled about the matter. He by his virtues might have borne the palm of holiness next to Wulstan; but he was in all things too severe. It is known that the blessed Bishop often broke off his merry talk if Elmer would not smile or checked him with a frown. Yet he was so consistent, so chaste, so temperate that envy could find nothing to strike at in him, friendship could not praise him too much. For this the Bishop did greatly reverence him and heard him say Mass daily with devout attention. For each of them so vied with the other in religious observance that they never let a day pass without the sacrifice of the Mass. Elmer therefore took the sick man into his house and comforted him with kind words. Moreover he bethought him of a way to win from the bishop by craft the miracle which he could not obtain openly. He found it by means of the water in which Wulstan had washed holy hands after the Mass. This Elmer gave to the servant aforesaid, and bade him pour it into the sick man's bath. The leper went into the water frightful to behold; his flesh full of sores. But, O wonder, straightway the swelling boils went down, the deadly matter ran away: and in a word, his flesh came again as the flesh of a little child. Even the scabs and blains on his head were banished, and his hair grew again thick and comely.

CHAPTER VIII

WULSTAN, journeying to London to the King's Court, came to a village called Wycombe, and there lodged in an old tottering house. In the morning when he was about to depart, the whole house began to creak and groan, and the beams and timbers were nodding to their fall. His servants in confusion rushed out of the house, forgetting that their lord was alone within, such blind terror had smitten their minds. And now they stood at the door and loudly cried to him to save himself by coming forth before the whole building fell. Not one of them was ready to risk his own life for Wulstan's safety, or dared to go in and fetch him out. But he, more calm for the greatness of the danger, rebuked their clamour: O ye of little faith, think ye that the fall of the house will crush me? he said; and would not set foot outside till he had seen the beasts of burden led forth. When he had come forth, straightway the whole house fell with a dreadful crash, walls and roof mingled in one heap of ruin. It was a wondrous and a goodly sign. As long as the Saint was within the house delayed its fall—when he came forth, it straightway crumbled and fell.

CHAPTER IX

COLEMAN sets down in this place a miracle which was wrought in this same town, in a later year, and still more notable. I have thought it well to bring together on the one page two events apart in time, alike in greatness. The miracle was on this manner. A man surnamed Swertlin, blessed with abounding riches, and full of reverence for the Saint, had built a Church at his own charges, and would have no man consecrate it but Wulstan. He held that it should not be dedicated till our Bishop dedicated it. But he was troubled and uncertain because that could not be done till the Bishop of that diocese had word of it. But his uncertainty was removed by Remigius, Bishop of Lincoln, who willingly granted his license. On the appointed day Bishop Wulstan came, and at the dedication of the Church he preached to the people and solemnly confirmed children. When service was done he went to dinner at Swertlin's house. The Lady of the house, from womanly modesty and reverence for the Bishop, was afraid to speak with him, so she told her trouble to Coleman. Her maid-servant suffered with a cruel disease, to wit, a monstrous tumour in her head: and her tongue thrust forth from her jaws and seemed more like the tongue of an ox than of a woman. She could eat no food, and if she took any into her mouth she could not chew it with her teeth: and they gave her to drink with a spoon. When the monk heard it he did his best for her, sending to the sick woman water which the saint had that day blessed for the consecration of the Church. Moreover he told the Bishop. Now the Bishop had one of those gold coins which we called besants from the city formerly Byzantium, now Constantinople. This coin had been thrust through with the spear which in the hand of a false persecutor pierced the side of Our Lord and Saviour. He dipped this besant in water and sent the water so hallowed to the maid. He had many times tried it and proved its healing power. The medicine quickly gave health, as the lady after some days declared to Coleman on her own oath and that of other witnesses.

CHAPTER X

HE was going from Worcester to one of his villages, riding last of the company, as he always did, that no one might break in upon his psalms with casual talk. As it chanced Coleman was riding near him. Meanwhile the Bishop spied a blind man crying from the roadside. He made a sign to the monk to give him an alms, for that, he supposed, was what he was asking. But the blind man, hoping in his heart for a far better thing, walked by Coleman's horse, and opened his grief. Would not Coleman pray the Bishop in God's name to stay awhile? It had been shown to him clearly in a dream that he could restore light to his eyes if he would. The worthy priest met the blind man's petition with ready assent. He told the matter to the Bishop, and added his own entreaties. The Bishop long drew back, and pleaded that he was not worthy to work miracles. But there was little that Coleman could not win from his kind heart—and he ceased not from pious violence and praiseworthy importunity till he had Wulstan dismounted from his horse. Then Wulstan repeated the Psalm *Ad te levavi*, and made the sign of the Cross over the eyes of the blind man, and went his way. A week passed; and Coleman returning to Worcester found the man whom he had left blind now seeing clearly. The miracle fired his heart, and the hearts of all that heard it to praise God: and loosed their tongues.

CHAPTER XI

ANOTHER like miracle he did at Wilton. He had gone thither either because he was so minded or because the road led that way: I know not. He was welcomed by the nuns with great joy and sat among them. There was in that convent a woman named Gunnilda daughter of King Harold of whom I spake above. A malignant tumour had attacked her eyes, so that the weight of her swollen eyelids blocked her sight. Her complaint came to the Bishop's ears, and he bade them fetch her. Wulstan, holding that he owed not a little to her father's memory, showed mercy worthy of himself, for his very heart was moved by her sufferings. So he made the sign of the Cross before her eyes, and, that I may not be longer in telling the miracle than he was in working it, straightway she was able to lift her eyelids and receive the light of day.

CHAPTER XII

KING WILLIAM had brought in a custom which the Kings that were after him followed for a while, and suffered to fall into disuse: to wit that thrice in the year all the great men of the realm should meet at the King's Court, to take counsel on the affairs of the kingdom, and to behold the King in his majesty wearing his crown set with precious stones. The places and times of the assembly are not to our present purpose. Obedient to this rule and custom our Bishop was faring to Winchester before Easter. There lay in his path a Frenchman sore vexed with pain in his bowels. He was writhing this way and that in agony, as a snake twists itself in coils; uttering pitiful cries and beating the air with doleful lamentations. Many passing by grieved over his suffering but could find no remedy. At last came Wulstan in a good time to ease him of his pains. When he heard the voice of the sufferer, and anon perceived that he had faith, he straightway dismounted: and his companions followed his example and sprang quickly to the ground. The sick man hearing the trampling of horses, asked some who could speak the French tongue what it was, and learned that it was the company of Bishop Wulstan. When he heard the name Wulstan, which was not unknown even among the French, he straightway took courage, and with all his might cried out that he must have his blessing. What he asked in faith was readily granted. Wulstan gave him to drink of holy water from a horn as he lay: bending his body to him, but with mind erect. The while charity comforted him with the draught, prayer was beating at the gate of heaven. The man stood up whole. With the last word of Wulstan's prayer his sickness departed from him. Thereafter Wulstan went on his way to Winchester and ended prosperously the journey which he had begun with a willing mind.

CHAPTER XIII

THERE is a village belonging to the diocese of Worcester which has from old time the name of Wich, where strange to tell salt pans are made from fresh water springs. There dwelt a woman, who was born neither to great wealth nor to abject poverty. She was married to a husband of the like middle fortune, and kept house as fitted their estate. But no prosperity abides unshaken: never does happiness smile on poor mortals without a cloud. Her easy life was marred by a sudden malady: a malady which seized not only on one member, but on every limb, and stiffened and knotted all her joints. Day by day she grew worse, and was forced to keep her bed. The poor woman, and her husband likewise sought such aid as they could afford from physicians. The physicians did their best and plied their craft, and what they could not do, they made up in promises—but all their consultations were to no purpose. Fortune made all their diligence of none effect—fortune, or as I would sooner believe, Divine Providence, perceiving that here was a task for his Bishop. And now all their store was spent; and the woman despairing of human aid fled for help to Christ: right wisely and prudently. For God Himself put the thought in her heart, and showed her in a vision that she should be delivered from that plague if she should prevail to get a letter from Bishop Wulstan. She had a son in the Bishop's household who had been committed for instruction to Coleman. Through him a message was carried, and in due time came to the ears of the Bishop. Frewin, at that time deacon and thereafter monk, an honest and cheerful fellow, brought these words written: *May Jesus Christ heal thee, Segild,* for so was she named. With lively faith she received the Bishop's gift, and anon made trial of its virtue. The scroll was first laid where the pain was severest and eased the pain. Soon the woman was altogether rid of her malady; and regained strength.

CHAPTER XIV

THE grace of miracles abounded in him for the Lord willed that the world should know how acceptable to Him was the obedience of his faithful servant. For all his life long he neglected the care of his body that he might follow after that which taught him to despise the things of the world and long earnestly for heavenly things. Whenever he went about his dioceses he never sent the people away without a Mass and a sermon. That he did constantly and diligently. He never broke his fast till he had signed with the Cross any number of children brought in from all the country round. This he did from daylight till dark—not only in winter but in summer. It is proved by good testimony that he often confirmed two thousand, sometimes three or more in one day: and that not only when he was young and vigorous, and the pleasure of well-doing drew him to the task, but also when age was beginning to sprinkle his head with snow, and his frail body could scarce keep pace with his eager soul. All men marvelled when eight clerks bearing the chrism sank down from weariness, while Wulstan continued unwearied. It was the love of God that made him unconscious of his labours, so that his mind yielded not to old age, but, though his body failed, came forth conqueror. This life he lived, as I have said, constantly fasting; but once at Gloucester he was persuaded by Abbot Serlo to break his rule. Masses had been duly said, and he was going out to the children, when the said Abbot begged him to honour the brethren's refectory with his presence that day. There were many reasons, he said, why he should not stiffly refuse —first, a little rest would be good for his health; secondly he should not seem to reject the good will of God's servants, to whose will the Lord Jesus Himself had at times gently yielded. Moreover the throng of children might meanwhile be disposed in ordered line, so that he could come and go among them more con-

Book II Chapter XIV

veniently. The Bishop was overcome by the Abbot's reasoning, and the earnest entreaties of all the monks. Meanwhile the common folk in the cemetery were talking and saying this and that as it came into their mouths. And one young man, prompted by the forwardness of youth, began to mock—Why do ye tarry for the Bishop who is filling his belly with the monks? Come: if any man would have his child signed, let him come to me. Therewith he took mud and smeared the face of the nearest infant, muttering unseemly words. The madness spread, and greeted his foolish act with cries of, Bind up that one's forehead, he has been signed; and wanton laughter—but it did not go unpunished. The people took the young man's saying and deed with a laugh—but the vengeance of heaven slept not, and would not lightly suffer God's gift and the reverence due to God's servant to be turned to mockery. Soon the guilty scorner fell to raving before them all. The devil who had tempted him to sin now drove him to frenzy. He tore his hair—he grinned—he beat his head against the wall. The people acclaimed the miracle, and praising God drove the maniac away. He wandered madly hither and thither with stumbling feet; and plunged into a well or pit hard by the cemetery. There he would have spued out his life, but his kinsmen drew him out with ropes and carried him to the inn. The Bishop was told of it: and grieved alike for the young man's fault and for his punishment. He sent him his blessing and the sufferer got back his wits. But I believe he died a few days later of what he had done or suffered in his madness.

CHAPTER XV

AGAIN Wulstan was bidden to Gloucester by the Abbot to dedicate a Church. A multitude of people thronged about him, seeking, as men will, remission of penances, and above all things desiring the Bishop's blessing. It rejoiced his heart exceedingly to behold the people flowing in to the service of God like a mighty river. Nor did he deny them streams of utterance, but poured it forth with abounding charity. He spent much of the day in preaching, freely putting into their hearts what he held it most concerned them to learn. Peace I mean—for mortal man can hear of nothing sweeter, seek nothing more to be desired, find nothing more precious. Peace, which is the beginning and end of man's salvation—the final purpose of God's commandments. The angel choir chanted it at the Incarnation; the Lord gave it to the disciples before His Crucifixion; and at His Resurrection brought it back to them as a trophy of victory. So spake Wulstan to the people: and confirmed his teaching with examples. But I am writing for lettered men; you know what I would say, and I need not give you instances. And indeed on that day many who were inplacable before consented to be reconciled. People urged one another to peace; and if any were still at variance they appealed to the Bishop. Thereat one William, surnamed the Bald, took heart to open his grief. He had slain a man, by chance not of malice: but he could not gain the friendship of the dead man's kindred on any terms, nor obtain pardon by the payment of any price. The

Book II Chapter XV

venerable Abbot had often tried to bring them to an agreement; but he had spent his labours in vain. There were five brothers, who breathed threatenings and slaughter for the death of their kinsman, enough to affright any man. Who would not tremble when he beheld five grown men, strong and fierce, seeking the life of one? They were brought to the Bishop, who besought them to pardon the man's misdeed; but they stoutly refused, saying angrily that they would sooner be utterly excommunicated than fail to avenge their brother. Then did God's priest, that he might in any way prevail with them, fall at their feet even as he was, clad in the sacred vesture of a Bishop. He renewed his entreaties stretched upon the ground, and promised for the dead man the benefit of Masses as well at Worcester as at Gloucester. All his great humility availed nothing, for they swore they would never be reconciled. Their brother's death had so vexed them that they had no longer the hearts of men. What rage indeed must have harassed them that they could scorn the white hairs tumbled in the dust, that even angels would, methinks, have revered. Moreover in their scorn of Wulstan they did wrong to God: human pride trampled underfoot the vesture of God's Bishop. Wherefore the prelate, having accomplished nothing by meekness, went on to meet a stubborn distemper with sterner medicine, saying that it was easy to discern between the children of God and the children of the Devil: for if one believe the truth, even as one must needs believe Him that spake it, *Blessed are the peacemakers for they shall be called the children of God,* then it is plain that they are the children of the Devil who strive against peace. For of whom one doeth the works of him is he called the son. The people cried aloud that so it was and so would they have it: and began to rail at the five brothers. Divine vengeance followed hard on the ill words of the people, and straightway one of the brothers, and that the fiercest, became mad. The wretch wallowed on the ground, gnawing the earth and tearing it with his fingers, foaming at the mouth; and, what I have never heard of before or since, smoke came from his limbs, so that the air about him was poisoned with the foul stench. What think you was then the mind of the four? Their swollen temper sank: their insolence departed: their pride withered. Then might you see them eagerly seeking what they had rejected: offering peace, pleading for mercy. Fear for themselves made them cringe: love for their brother taught them meekness. For they thought that on them as on him might fall vengeance for the crime of which all alike were guilty. Their humbled bearing moved the tender heart of the Bishop, and after Mass he granted healing to the sufferer, relief from fear to the others, and peace to all.

CHAPTER XVI

SO it came about that no man dared gainsay Wulstan when he preached peace. He was a father who rejoiced when his sons advanced in wisdom and goodness; for he knew that their soul's health was unto him great gain; so, as it were for his own profit, he ever bade them press on to good works, being, as saith the apostle, *instant in season, out of season, with all long-suffering and doctrine.* And if he could not conveniently preach, as befell in his last years, when his legs pained him: he would bid Coleman preach in his place—for he prized Coleman for the cleanness of his life, the dignity of his presence, the readiness of his speech, and the aptness of his learning. But, for all that, he could not attain unto the grace given to Wulstan that the people heard him gladly. For when the Bishop spake of peace all men hung upon his words. Not so with Coleman. When he preached they murmured or departed. Nevertheless in this matter the vengeance of heaven justified the priest, that all men might learn to honour the Bishop in honouring his ministers. There was in Worcester a labouring man named Ermer, the kind of mason called a plasterer. He had a murderous hate against one of the same town: and whenever he heard Coleman speak of peace, he straightway went forth of the Church, and bade farewell to sermon and monk at once. Meanwhile he flattered himself, and comforted his heart with the thought that it was not the Bishop preaching; and because it was only a monk speaking he might safely despise his counsel. Not so it seemed to God. For not long after the scaffold brake on which this same workman was standing to lay stones, and a sore evil befell him that never left him; for he was lamed in both his legs. For a year he lay upon his bed, and never again walked like a whole man. His punishment was a lesson to many: and no man thereafter dared refuse when bidden in Wulstan's name to be at peace with his neighbour.

CHAPTER XVII

THERE was nothing that Wulstan more carefully avoided than falling into anger or speaking too harshly when he was vexed by the sins of his people. Not that he fell easily into either fault—or, if he did, it was with good cause, as shall presently appear. One Ailsi, who had been a servant of King Edward, called the Bishop to his village, Longney-on-Severn, to consecrate a Church: and he came, never tarrying over such a duty. The place was too strait for the people, who had run together in multitudes to Wulstan, as they were wont. Hard by in the churchyard was a nut tree with wide shady leafage, which by the unpruned spread of its branches darkened the Church. The Bishop sent for his host, and bade him cut it down. It was fitting, he said, that if Nature had not given room for the Church man's industry should provide it. It was not fitting that what Nature had given man should use for wantonness. For Ailsi used to sit under that tree, especially in summer, dicing and drinking, and amusing himself with other games. Wherefore, far from obeying meekly, he stubbornly refused. And, as he afterwards confessed, he vowed in his mad impudence that he would sooner not have the Church consecrated at all than cut down his tree. Then the saint greatly moved at his perverseness, hurled his curse at the tree. The tree was stricken thereby, and gradually became barren and bare no fruit and withered from the roots. Its unfruitfulness so vexed the owner, that whereas he had jealously possessed it and loved it dearly, he now grew sick of its barrenness, and bade it be cut down. This same good man told Coleman when he came thither again, that he held it for certain and said it that nothing could be found more bitter than Wulstan's curse: nothing sweeter than Wulstan's blessing.

CHAPTER XVIII

MANY a time were those punished by Heaven who perversely troubled the peace of his soul. Here is an instance. He had come soon after Easter to a village named Blockley. It was the day of the Octave, the day on which Our Lord after His Resurrection wrought again a miracle, and brought His true Body unto the upper room when the doors were shut. Wulstan was about to say Mass, and was vexed to find the ornaments of the Altar unworthy of the Feast—guttered candles in common candlesticks, and the linen long unwashed. So he nodded to a server to run to the Chamberlain and bid him put all right. But that servant, who had often presumed on the good nature of the kind Bishop, fell into a rage and boxed the boy's ears; and he ran weeping to his Master and told him. The Bishop's heart burned with anger against his insolent servant, and his countenance was changed; but he kept it within his breast, and passed over the matter for the time in perfect silence. But, marvellous to tell, in that same hour when anger shook the mind of the Bishop in Church, sickness smote the body of the serving man in his chamber. Stricken, he fell to the ground, and almost ceased to breathe. Of a surety he lost all sense and feeling. He lay like a man at the point of death. Colour fled from his face, warmth from his body, speech from his lips. Men ran to him as he lay, and sought a cause for his sudden fall until they found it. Because he had struck the innocent child, the Bishop had been angry; and the man was now paying the penalty of his sacriligeous daring. His pardon must be obtained from him for whose sake the misdeed had found its punishment. The business was committed to a monk whom I have often named, and he carried to Wulstan a message from them all. Straightway his blessing was granted, and healing followed confession as swiftly as sickness had fallen upon sin.

CHAPTER XIX

I SHALL now come to a miracle which, being wrought in our own days, does not easily find believers. Coleman knowing it would be so has supported it with many witnesses lest the faith of hearers should waver, and unbelief prevail. And indeed when he first brought the news of it to Worcester, some accused him of lying, saying peevishly that it was not truth he cared for but the greater glory of the Saint. But he maintained it the more earnestly, bringing forward as lawful witnesses many men of repute. Nor did he cease till he had bruised the gainsayers' foreheads of brass, in as much as men worthy of trust declared, yea and swore by all that is holy, that they had tested the truth of it. It fell on this wise: there is a seaport town called Bristol, from which it is a straight voyage to Ireland, so that it is a convenient port for the barbarous people of that island. Some Bristol men and other English were sailing to Ireland, as was their wont, with merchandise. And now they had put forth into the deep, when the face of the sky was changed, and the light of day gave place to the darkness of night. The tempest raged, the rain poured down: it was as though the world was being broken up. You might have thought the winds were fighting for the destruction of the unlucky sailors. The ropes parted, the mast broke, the oars were carried away: the ship was drifting unguided at the mercy of chance. The sailors could only look for death, and for three days and nights dragged on a wretched existence, without food or sleep. Dear God, the misery of the poor men with the fear of death upon them. For methinks it is less hard to die swiftly like a man, than to wait for a craven's end. On the fourth day when all spirit was departing from them, God, who would not the death of the wretched but their life, put it into the heart of one of them to say, Ye that are of the bishopric of the right reverend Wulstan, why do ye not pray the pity of God, that by his intercession he may bring us out of this sore peril? The others caught up the word from his mouth, and with one voice poured forth their very hearts in prayer. And anon the loving mercy of the Almighty raised up them that lay in darkness, and the shadow of death, showing to them not, as I hold, very Wulstan, but the present image and semblance of him. Marvellous it may be to relate, but what so many good men declare cannot but be true. He went about the ship, making fast the tackling, splicing the ropes; calling now on one man, now on the whole crew. Take heart, he said, hoist the yards, belay the halliards and sheets; and by God's good will and my aid you will soon reach the land. As he promised so it came to pass. They were soon in a harbour of Ireland: and not long after returned with fair winds to England, and told the miracle abroad in all places. We should well believe that what God has done not once nor twice by saints of old, that He may have done in our own time, seeing that we read how certain holy men, sometimes knowing what they did, sometimes not knowing, succoured those who were afar off; and though absent in body, yet appeared as they would in the spirit. I name them not that I may not seem to borrow from another man's store.

CHAPTER XX

THIS miracle had such power with the men of Bristol that they were wholly minded to do whatsoever Wulstan bade them. And at the last he removed from among them a very ancient custom, which was so rooted in their hearts that neither the love of God nor the fear of King William had yet prevailed to do away with it. For they used to buy men from all England and carry them to Ireland in the hope of gain; nay, they even set forth for sale women whom they had themselves gotten with child. You might well groan to see the long rows of young men and maidens whose beauty and youth might move the pity of a savage, bound together with cords, and brought to market to be sold. It was a damnable sin, a piteous reproach, that men, worse than brute beasts, should sell into slavery their own lemans, nay, their own blood. This long-established custom, come down from their forefathers, Wulstan, as I have said, blotted out little by little. He knew them for a stiff-necked generation, hard to bend; so he would sojourn in their coasts two months or three together. Each Sunday he would come to Bristol, and by his preaching sow the good seed, which in due time sprang up and bore fruit—so that not only did they forsake their sin, but were an example to all England. One of them, who stubbornly transgressed the counsel of the Bishop, they cast out of the city and blinded his eyes. Therein I praise their goodwill, but blame their deed. But when the minds of rough men are once stirred, no force of reason can withstand them.

CHAPTER XXI

AT the bidding of King William and Archbishop Thomas, Wulstan once was on his way to York before Easter to bless the Chrism, and came to Nottingham, a notable town on no mean river, the Trent, which can be crossed there. He sent on his servants to provide lodging for his whole company. The Sheriff, as it chanced, was from home: but his good wife honourably received the messengers, the more that they were Wulstan's men. For the repute of his holiness had come like a gentle breeze to her ears also. She did not wholly believe nor wholly disbelieve what she had heard concerning him. She scarce knew what to believe. Therefore she spoke to his forerunners and questioned them straitly, and besought them in the name of God, to deliver her from doubt whether the Bishop's holiness truly matched the report of it. Frewin answered truly and modestly, neither abating aught nor aught exaggerating. The Bishop, he said, gave himself gladly and simply to God's service—that was what he loved in himself and in others. The lady went deeper with her questioning, seeking to draw down an answer from heaven. Wulstan, she said, would be made manifest as a servant of God, if fish came to the nets to mend his fare. For three months past no fish at all had been taken at Nottingham. So let Him loose the knot of her uncertainty Who had confirmed the faith of doubting Thomas by the marks of the nails. This she said to herself. But having entertained the messengers right hospitably she sent her servants to fish, leaving the issue to the decision of chance. Forthwith the fishermen, who, as I said, had toiled long and caught nothing, took five huge salmon in their nets. But, being men who thought little of a lie if they gained by it, they stole the three largest, and brought the two to their mistress. She came, dancing with joy, to the lord Bishop and told the whole story. No longer could she doubt that he was filled with the grace of God. Earnestly she besought him that he would vouchsafe to her the benefit of being remembered in his prayers. So much on the first day: on the next the falsehood of the thieves was revealed and the other three salmon brought in, which made the marvel greater. For this too she held must be accounted to his holiness that God would not suffer him to be cheated of any part of His bounty: and she added moreover a goodly gift. Here it is good and pleasant to mark how ready was the spirit of prophecy in him as now shall notably appear.

CHAPTER XXII

ONE Sewi, a man of great riches, had built a church on his estate of Ratcliffe. He, greatly desiring that it should be dedicated by Wulstan, had sought and obtained a licence from the Archbishop of York. The rumour had gone abroad that Wulstan should discharge the duty of dedicating it: and the people came thronging to the Church. Wulstan was long in preaching, and as he was wont, spake to the people of peace and goodwill. Whereat a certain poor man took heart and hope to stand forth. With many prayers he besought the Bishop to make peace between him and a certain rich man who was standing by. Coleman leaves out both their names, whether of set purpose or because he had forgotten them; but he saith that the rich man was a priest, but love of gain had made him false to his priesthood. Wulstan called him forth and twice and thrice entreated him to a peace; but he scornfully set at naught his entreaties. Then did Wulstan take up his prophecy against the proud man before him. I will not fail to give his very words. Thou wilt not have peace, he said: Verily I say unto you the hour cometh and now is that thou shalt desire to have mercy on him and on others, and shalt not be able. Thou shalt seek for mercy and it shall be denied thee. The rich priest was not a whit moved by his words, but departed in haste to his own house. But Fortune that had so long played pander to him now turned a scorpion tail against him: and brought in his foes upon him—whereat his companions fled whither they might: and he was slain and proved the truth of the prophecy to his cost. The thing was an example for others, if ever mortals can be taught to see what belongeth unto their health, that they should not dare to transgress the precepts of holy men.

Here ends the Second Book.

Here begins the Third Book.

CHAPTER I

HITHERTO I have told, and that gladly, of Wulstan's miracles; few of them, but enough to bear witness to his holiness. Now I will essay to speak of his daily life and conversation. And first concerning his habit of body. He was of the middle stature, lower than some men, higher than others; well formed and well proportioned in all parts. The calmness of his mind suited with the comeliness of his body so that he won the reverence of all men. He ever had sound health which his sparing use of food and sleep helped not a little. In his raiment, his bed furniture, and his shoes, he was neither over sumptuous nor niggardly. He eschewed pride this way and that; for there can be boasting in filthy rags. Yet he inclined rather to what is humble, that he might fall short in outward show, not in grace. So avoiding all ostentation, even when he was a rich man, he would wear only lamb-skins. Hence it came to pass that on a day Geoffrey, Bishop of Coutances, chid him friendly, showering on him merry jests. He asked him why he would still wear lambskins, when he could and should have sable or beaver or wolf. Wulstan answered with a good grace that Geoffrey and men versed in worldly prudence should use the fur of cunning beasts: he for his simplicity was content with lambskin. Geoffrey had at him again and bade him at least put on catskin. Believe me, quoth Wulstan, we sing the Lamb of God oftener than the Cat of God. Geoffrey laughed, well pleased that he should have the worse of the jest, and that Wulstan could not be over-persuaded.

CHAPTER II

EXCEPT when he went into refectory with the monks, Wulstan would always dine publicly in hall with his knights: for he held it unseemly and ungracious to dine alone and have his servants murmuring at it; although from the day he put on the religious habit and for some years before that, he never allowed himself rich dishes, but said good-bye to fat things and all flesh save of fish. It will not be amiss to recall the occasion on which he laid upon himself this rule. Bishop Brihtheah, as I have told you, had advanced him from minor orders to the priesthood, and thereon had committed to him the church of Hawkesbury.

Wulstan was then barely come to manhood, yet he did not give thought to the pleasures of the world as a young man might. Meanwhile he did not altogether eschew savoury meats, and one day he ordered a goose to be roasted. The fowl was spitted and roasting, carefully tended by a scullion. In the heat of the fire the dripping began to run from it. Some of the servants were putting hot coals under. Some were making ready the sauce. The savoury smell made their mouths run with water; they could not refrain from saying how good it was. Even Wulstan was ensnared, and his soul melted in delight, as it were foretasting the goose. And now the table was all but laid, when he and his steward were called forth from the house on a business which came untimely but could not be delayed. So he went empty away; and began to find a fault in his lust of a moment. How weak was the flesh that could so be tempted to evil. The pleasure passed quickly away: the sin remained. He exacted from himself this penalty, that he should pay for the inordinate desire of one hour by perpetual abstinence. He made a vow and kept it that he would never again eat that kind of food. There were set before him fish and sauces, milk, cheese, and butter, whereof he sometimes partook; but more gladly ate only herbs. He would have edifying books read at his table, and silence was kept that all might hearken: and when men had well eaten he would expound what had been read in the vulgar tongue, that he might impart heavenly food to them for whose bodily sustenance he had already made provision. After dinner, when the rest had ale or mead set before them to drink, as is the English custom, Wulstan would drink pure water, though only his servant knew it, and others supposed it was some more costly brewage. All his earlier years he drank only water: when he grew old, he mingled with it some ale or wine.

CHAPTER III

HE kept a strict discipline over his house, as well laymen as clerks, for he made it a rule that all the men of his household should be at Mass and at all the Hours. He appointed men to see that none should escape who broke the rule. An offender lost his drink for the day, or was beaten on the hand with a rod. He never sent out one of his lay servants but he bade him pray seven times in the day. For he said it was fitting that if clerks offered seven hour offices to God, laymen should offer seven prayers. If any man swore in his presence, he was straightway beaten. And in his sermons he often warned the people not to fall into the habit of swearing, lest it should lead to false swearing. Moreover he was angry if any man in his presence slandered another, for he accounted it a very wicked thing. At night, when he had taken a little sleep, he would rise straightway. Then he would repeat psalms, or read in a book of prayers which he used no less than the Psalter and always carried in his bosom, or say the hours of the Blessed Virgin. Often he did this alone, that he might not stay others from their rest. Sometimes with a companion if he found one more wakeful than his fellows. And one night a certain Edric, whom

I also knew, sat with him as he said his office. But when Wulstan would not abate aught of his accustomed task, Edric grew tired of his long psalms and prayers, and dared to sign with his hand to the Bishop that he should cease. Wulstan rebuked his drowsiness with a look: and Edric sat down against his will, kept on nodding, and at last let himself go to sleep. But he was punished for his rashness, being sorely smitten in a vision, and scourged. And it was only when he pledged himself never to let or hinder a good man in a good work that he was delivered from the peril of that dreadful vision.

CHAPTER IV

WULSTAN would always sing Matins in a Church, however far the Church might be from his lodging. To Church he would go, snow or rain, storm or tempest. He would struggle over the worst of roads, if only he might come to the Church and say truly to God, '*Lord, I have loved the honour of Thine House.*' Once he was travelling to the King's Court before Christmas, and was lodged at Marlow. According to his custom he told his servants early in the morning that he was going to the Church. It was far off, and the road so deep in mire that it might have stayed a traveller even by daylight. Moreover there was a raging storm of snow and rain mingled to hinder him. His clerks dreaded the foul weather; but he was resolved, and would not be turned back. He would go to the Church, with one attendant or even alone if they would show him the road that he might not wander out of the way. Seeing that the Bishop's will withstood them, the clerks ceased from angry murmuring and held their peace. But Frewin, yet more froward than rest, took his lord's hand, and doubled his fault by leading him where the mire was deepest and the road most perilous. Wulstan was plunged in mud to the knees, and lost one of his shoes: but he did not show that he perceived their knavery. For the purpose of the clerks had been that the Bishop should weary of his resolve, and at last fall in with their counsel. It was now broad day, and he returned half dead with cold to the inn. Then at last he spake openly of what he had suffered by their naughtiness. He bade them find his lost shoe: and gently rebuked the impudent clerk, dismissing his offence with a smile. For the Lord Bishop was full of longsuffering. Wherewith he had so armed his mind that no disappointment could move him, no annoyance hurry him into doing wrong. For often some of his clerks spake openly against him, or jested on him in secret. But against this and all that came upon him from the world without he stood undaunted, so that although he was ware of it in his heart never did he offend with his lips. I will not claim for him the praise which I cannot establish that he was not moved to anger in his heart. For the thoughts of a man's heart no religion can ever dout. It may restrain them for the time, but it cannot take them away for ever.

CHAPTER V

HE heard at least two Masses daily; and at each made his oblation: and sang a third Mass himself. When he was travelling he would begin the psalter as he mounted his beast and paused not till the end. To this he added Litanies with many Collects; and Vigils and Vespers of the dead. If the journey was still prolonged, he repeated the psalms of the hours. His clerks and monks rode with him ready to take up the alternate verses, or to help his memory if he seemed to stumble. This he bade them do that they might avoid idle talking which so easily comes in the way of men on a journey. For then many things take the eye, and there is the more to talk of. His chamberlain rode by him, bearing a purse which was the common treasury of all needy folk. For no man who asked an alms of Wulstan ever had to complain of denial. When the day's journey was done, and they came to their lodging, he would never, as I have said, enter his chamber till he had saluted the Church with prayers. He bade a priest purge all the rooms of the lodging with holy water and the sign of the Cross. So, he said, should hostile powers be driven away, and friendly powers brought in.

CHAPTER VI

HE was ever praying or preaching if time allowed. If not, he was yearning godward, his mind fixed on heaven. When he was lying, standing, walking, sitting, there was ever a psalm in his mouth, ever

Christ in his heart. Sometimes worn out with overmuch labour of prayer he would lie down, and so far yield to nature as to sleep. But as soon as he awaked of himself or was roused by another, he began a Psalm, *Conserva me Domine*, or *Diligam te Domine*, or the like which breathe a prayer. In summer after dinner he would often lie on his bed; but, strange to relate, he could not fall asleep, unless one read to him. While the reader continued, he seemed to slumber, if the reader ceased, he straightway awoke. He would have read to him the Lives of Saints and other edifying writings. You might truly say that his life was a kind of heavenly mirror which gave back the express image of Saintliness. That it was a mirror of the divine pleasure—showing forth whatsoever things are holy, whatsoever things are profitable to salvation, whatsoever things are of good report.

CHAPTER VII

THEM that came to him to confess their sins he joyfully received, and dealt tenderly with them. He heard their confessions with most gracious kindness, and did not spurn them. He was ready to weep over their sins, and did not shrink from them as too grievous. So it came to pass that men from all England did not blush to confess to him what they would have entrusted to no other confessor. They were not ashamed to tell him what they were bitterly vexed at having done. He repaid his penitents with like good-will, earnestly bidding them not despair, and teaching them how to avoid sin in the future, and atone for the sins they had committed. I know not whether it be worthy of greater or less praise that he ever held in closer friendship those whose sins and penances were known to him.

CHAPTER VIII

HE was diligent in providing for the poor, making them sit before him by companies, and ministering abundantly to their needs. The sons of rich men who were being trained in his household, served him at table as is the custom. He filled their minds with wholesome precepts, bidding them put away pride and put on humility, and above all to keep innocency, lest in the wantonness of youth they should mire their bodies in the slough of concupiscence. He made them wait upon the table of the poor men with bent knee, and pour water on their hands like servants: and if one of them betrayed his pride of noble blood by so much as a look, he was chidden for insolence. Wulstan could forgive any offence rather than a contemptuous glance that might wound a poor man. They must observe the Lord's command to be servants of the poor: for he that giveth to the poor doth reverence to the Lord, who said: *In as much as ye did it unto one of the least of these My brethren ye have done it unto Me.* They were young, and sons of rich men, with the added grace of health to make them glad; but a change of fortune might make them of sad countenance: and then they would rejoice if any man came near to them and deigned to look on them. With such wise counsels did their pious teacher bring down the haughtiness of their young hearts that they might grow up to show reverence to the needy. Well favoured youths he would fondle with holy hands and kiss, embracing in them the beauty of God's handiwork and drew a moral from their comeliness saying how lovely must the Creator be who maketh such lovely creatures.

CHAPTER IX

IN every one of his Manors he had a little room wherein he shut himself after Mass and locked the door. There he found solitude as in a wilderness, and meditated on the vanity of the world and the nature of God. There was nothing to break in upon his thoughts, save when a clerk knocked on the door to warn him that it was time for dinner or an office. And the passage between his chamber and the private room was known only to his servants that he might not seem to make a show of religion. So he would be alone in the midst of men at all seasons, but chiefly in the season of Lent; that he might steal an hour in the body from the world which he ever shunned in the soul. For he was, as Nicholas, the venerable Prior of Worcester has told me, not only often in prayer but most earnest therein. When he came to a verse in the psalms which could stir his desire for God, such as *Incline thine ear, O Lord, and hear me, for I am poor and in misery*, or the like, he would say it over twice or thrice, lifting up his eyes to heaven. The Prior told me that he was careful of constancy in prayer not only for himself but for his household. If his rule were transgressed he would pass it over or rebuke it as occasion served. If he saw that one of the monks was not at Matins, he would say nothing at the time, but when the others were sleeping after the Office, he would gently rouse the defaulter, and make him pay his debt, himself saying the responses as the monk chanted. Surely a most wonderful man, a most humble bishop. He did not terrify the sleeper with kicks and threats; but he could not suffer the monk's offence to be lightly passed over, and made him earn pardon for his fault. Here he showed himself a faithful admonisher, there a good comrade; in both a gracious and godly bishop. I shall gladly tell more of the excellent Nicholas, if I can first set forth what I have to say concerning the life of Wulstan.

CHAPTER X

HE was, as I have said, most careful in visiting his diocese, without neglecting anything that belonged to his office. To do this more conveniently he set himself a bound each year, taking thought for his own health and the weariness of those who were to meet him. As he made his way through the whole bishopric after due notice from the archdeacons, such multitudes came about him as cannot be numbered. It was no light labour to minister to their necessities, but his strong spirit bore the burden and overcame the toil. In parishes which were on his own lands he built churches, in others he caused them to be built. There was at Westbury an ancient church, half fallen, half unroofed, in sore need of repair. He rebuilt it from the foundation upward, mending the walls with hewn stone, the roof with lead. He endowed it with glebe and tithes and furnished it with Office books, and by a formal deed of gift presented it to the Church of Worcester: and placing monks in it made Coleman Prior. Indeed he was so busy and eager in building houses of God, that he might even seem slack and careless about secular buildings. For in his manors he never built halls or banqueting rooms. Indeed it was not only in these habitations, but even in Churches that he was little pleased with laboured and curious work. For he thought that belonged rather to man's pomp and pride than to God's will and grace. This, Nicholas tells us, he showed on the day when he had the old Church of Worcester pulled down. He stood in the Churchyard silent and groaning in spirit. For his mind was filled with a thought which at last brake forth in a flood of tears. We poor wretches, he said, destroy the work of Saints, vainly supposing that we can do better. How much more excellent than we was S. Oswald who built this Church. How many holy men of religion have served God in it. And when they who stood by bade him not be sad, but rather rejoice that God had preserved him for the grace of beholding the Church so glorified, he would still be weeping. And some say that he foretold the burning of the new church, which befell in after years. But one must not take that for true, for the truth is not so; so let it rest there. But he did make a new church: nor could one easily find any goodly ornament that was lacking in it: so marvellous was it in every part, and in all together perfect above all other. And that nothing might be wanting to its splendour he set apart seventy-two marks of silver, for a shrine wherein he laid the body of S. Oswald that was bishop before him, and relics of many other saints. This was done in the presence of a great assembly, and Bishop Robert and certain Abbots on the eighth day of October, on which day it was commanded that the translation of the Saint aforesaid should be observed, and on the Octave the memorial of all those relics. This was so devised because the feast of the deposition of S. Oswald which falls in Lent cannot be so conveniently kept. The reader is to know that this shrine was made by Aldulf,[1] and enlarged by Wulstan.

CHAPTER XI

WULSTAN was so concerned for the estate of the souls of the faithful departed, that he constantly forbade men to ride at random through churchyards. Many bodies of the saints, he said, lie there and we should pay reverence to their souls which are with God. But all his pains availed little, seeing that even to this day the reverence due to departed saints is trampled underfoot. Whenever and wherever, as I have said above, he heard of any man's death, he straightway bade those present say a Paternoster, and himself repeated three Psalms, *Laudate dominum omnes gentes, De profundis,* and *Laudata dominum in Sanctis,* with

[1] *Note.* It is Oswald in the text, clearly an error.

Collects. And when he had prayed for the soul, he would speak awhile of the departed, in few words or at length as time served. He had a Mass for the dead sung each day except on Sundays and the greater feasts. He was content to forego the pious duty in honour of the festival, trusting that he should be the better heard inasmuch as he forebore asking. The daily prayer was sweet: that it was not offered on Sunday filled him with hope. Neither day would God rob him; for the divine clemency was well pleased when His servant praised Him by trusting Him.

CHAPTER XII

THE sin of incontinence he abhorred, and approved continence in all men, and especially in clerks in holy orders. If he found one wholly given to chastity he took him to himself and loved him as a son. Wedded priests he brought under one edict, commanding them to renounce their fleshly desires or their churches. If they loved chastity, they might remain and be welcome: if they were the servants of bodily pleasures, they must go forth in disgrace. Some there were who chose rather to go without their churches than their women: and of these some wandered about till they starved: others sought and at last found some other provision. A few, taking the wiser way, honourably grew old in their benefices. The Bishop, to avoid future scandal, would not thereafter ordain to the priesthood any who was not sworn to celibacy.

CHAPTER XIII

HE showed his humility everywhere, but especially among his monks. When he was at Worcester, he would say High Mass almost daily, and that more often of his own motion, than because he was asked by the monk whose week it was. He was wont to say, as Nicholas tells us, that he was a monk of that House and owed his week to the Church like the rest: and, because he could not discharge his duty in his turn, he must do it when he was there present. He was often at the reading of holy books; and then having made his confession, and given the blessing, returned to his own house. At early dawn while others slept, he would come into the Church, and if one of the brethren, as sometimes happened, wanted to say his Mass and had no server, Wulstan would serve him. When he saw choir boys or others untidy in their dress, he would stoop down and make the folds hang straight and smooth, out the wrinkles.

CHAPTER XIV

WHEN he was told that the humility he loved was beneath the dignity of a bishop, he would answer, *He that is greater among you shall be your servant.* I am your Bishop and master: and therefore ought I to be servant of you all, according to the Lord's precept. For never did he bow to the judgment of his own will, but in all things followed the precepts of the Lord. He was right pleasant in his ways, never offending them that dwelt with him by harshness, never by ingratitude putting to shame them who would serve him. He often retrenched from his own state to make provision for the well-being of his people: yet in all things spoke and acted as became the office of a bishop. And that not only in Worcester, but wherever in the diocese he was bidden to a religious house. For it was not his way to keep them that bade him waiting for an answer or frame excuses for delays in coming. Whenever he was told that there were children to be confirmed he straightway rose to fulfil the desire of them that asked him. If he was waking, he put aside what he had in hand: if he was sleeping, he rose forthwith from sleep. The altars at that time were of wood, as they had been from the beginning in England. These he did away throughout the diocese and built others of stone. So it came to pass that he would dedicate two altars in one day in some village, and as many on the morrow and the third day in other places. Wherever he was needed there he was to be found; so quickly that he seemed rather to fly than to travel. And a miracle that he so wrought at a dedication I will not suffer to go unrecorded.

CHAPTER XV

WHILE he was going about dedicating altars, he came near to a place where Ailric the Archdeacon had newly built a Church. The Bishop, knowing that it was ready to be dedicated, called the Archdeacon to him as the evening was falling. Go, he said, and make all ready for the consecration of the Church.

I will come at dawn and be with you for the ceremony. Ailric grew pale at the sudden command, but could offer no excuse save that he had not made due provision. So great a company would need much victual. He himself would be content with little; but he feared the importunity of his friends. Go, said the Bishop, do thy part. God will find meat for his servants. Seeing we are nigh unto the place we will do God's work. The Archdeacon could not choose but hasten away and make all ready for the consecration: and moreover of his bounty he prepared all things needful for a feast. Only he had no mead, save a small vessel that he had begged from his friends. So the Bishop came, and having done that wherefor he had come, was about departing. The Archdeacon and his friends turned him from his purpose and persuaded him to abide there for that day. After dinner the host's hospitable soul bade him give all his guests to drink from the vessel aforesaid. The mead held its own with the drinkers: and as if it poured from a spring abounded the more the more they drew from it. You would have believed it was the barrel of meal and the cruse of oil wherefrom the widow of Sarepta was fed by him who had asked her for food. Methinks it was a greater work of Grace; for there three souls were kept alive; here a multitude had enough and to spare. And, marvel upon marvel, three days after the vessel was found half full though all it held seemed barely enough for that great company. Nor did the Archdeacon hold his peace: but told it abroad as a proof of the Bishop's tender care for his people.

CHAPTER XVI

NOW that strong drink has come into my tale, I will tell a strange thing that befell one who drank when Wulstan had forbidden it. He had in his household many knights; not because it pleased him or flattered him to have a great retinue about him, for his heart did not take pride in the multitude of his servants: but King William had commanded that it should be so, for there was a common report that the Danes were coming and would be here anon. And truly they would have come, but other matters stayed them. Why they threatened and what held them back I have set forth in my *Gesta Regum Anglorum* where the friendly reader will find it. For this cause the King was afraid and called together his council to make provision against the danger. The whole council were of one mind with Lanfranc that the households of great men should be strengthened with knights, that if the occasion arose, they might join in one host to guard the common weal and their own weal against the barbarian. So our Bishop had a company of knights who were well paid, and fared sumptuously. And one day they were feasting more bounteously than was their wont, and at the first they grew merry in their cups; then fell to talking as men do at a banquet; and from talking came to quarrelling, and from quarrelling near to fighting. Thereat the Bishop was troubled and somewhat wrath. He bade the cupbearers to cease hurrying to and fro, and commanded that no man should drink in his house that day. They all obeyed save Nicholas, who, because he stood high in the Bishop's favour, dared to enter the cellar and transgress the command. Then he went to his bed, and being troubled with frightful dreams began to utter strange cries. Coleman who was sleeping near by awoke him and asked the cause of all his trouble. He (far be it from Christian men) answered that he was grievously vexed by a devil, and could find no rest for that he had been disobedient to the Bishop. But his fellows persuaded him to dispel the phantasm by prayer and the sign of the Cross, and he fell asleep again. Yet again and for the third time he endured the like or worse terrors—and perceived at last that the only remedy was to gain the pardon of him whom he had disobeyed to his own hurt. Wulstan, as his custom was, was praying alone in the Church. Nicholas fell at the good father's feet, and confessed his fault: and Wulstan blessed him graciously and healed him of his distemper.

CHAPTER XVII

AND here let the memory of this venerable servant find a place in the pages of his master's life. Nicholas was of a noble English stock. His parents had a great reverence for Wulstan, and did many things to gain his friendship. He himself baptized the child Nicholas, had him liberally instructed, and as he grew to manhood kept him ever close at his side. Anon, that he might be perfected in learning, he sent him into Kent to serve a while under Lanfranc's discipline. Afterwards, in the time of Bishop Thiulf he was made Prior of Worcester, and in a little space proved himself diligent in his office. What I hold right profitable is that by teaching and example he did so drive letters into the monks of that place that, though they be fewer in number than the greatest Churches of England, they are no whit behind them in learning. Nicholas loved to tell the sayings and doings of Wulstan, and is peradventure to be blamed that he did not set them down in writing. For no man could have recorded them more exactly since none knew him more closely. Even his chance sayings had some weight, as this: He was stroking with fatherly kindness the head of Nicholas whose hair was beginning to go back from his brow and leave it bare. The young man jesting with the Bishop said, Full well dost thou keep my locks which are all departing. Wulstan answered, Believe me thou shalt not be bald as long as I live, and so it fell out—for in the very week that Wulstan's spirit left the earth all that was left of Nicholas's hair likewise scattered to the winds.

CHAPTER XVIII

EVERY day in Lent, the reader remembers he washed the feet and hands of poor men, and gave them an allowance of food. This he did rather by night than by day, shunning the judgments of men which are ever partial, running to overmuch love or hatred. And if there sat among them one afflicted with the King's Evil, Wulstan would be handling his feet longer, kissing him more tenderly, and gazing at his sores. On

Maundy Thursday he spent the whole day until night continually in such pious works. And whereas he was ever wholly given to the worship of God, on that day he took great pains that nothing worldly should creep into his doings. When he had sung Matins with his monks in choir, he went back to his chamber and found hot water and napkins set ready by the servants whose duty it was. Then having washed the feet of a number of poor men, he clothed them moreover in new raiment from head to foot, ministering his charity with his own hands. Then he rested for a little while, and his servants filled the great hall with poor persons, setting them in ranks as close as ever they could sit. To every one of them the Bishop gave shoes and a meal with his own hands—and if any said to him, My lord, rest now, thou hast well done, he answered, I have done but little, but I have the will to do my Lord's command. Then he departed into the Church, and all day until None withdrew himself from the world and yearned to heaven. Then followed the reconciliation of penitents, the celebration of Mass and the blessing of the Chrism. All this Coleman describes at great length, but I have chosen to leave it out, because my purpose is not to set down what belongs to the office of a bishop, but to write the life of Wulstan. For what does it serve to say what other Bishops do, and must needs do as it is set down for them in the books? One thing I must not pass over—that his countenance to penitents was so full of grace that when they looked on it with their eyes they thought in their hearts that it was an angel of God. For instinct teaches us to hope for remission of our sins through one in whom we find no offence at all. On that day, Wulstan would eat with the reconciled penitents; and after supper he washed the feet of all the monks, and served cups of wine to them with a kiss, as we have heard. Thus from one midnight till far into the darkness of the next night he was wont to withdraw himself from the world.

CHAPTER XIX

IN the year before his death he did so effectually provide the Maundy ceremony, that his diligence in former years might seem as nothing. He foresaw doubtless that he was doing it for the last time, and outdid all his servants by a miracle of anxious care. He bade each of his reeves to provide from each of his manors full raiment for one man, shoes for ten men, and victuals for a hundred. He bade his chamberlains make like provision that what his estates could not find his household should supply. Thrice that day the great hall was filled with poor persons, so closely packed that one could scarce move forward, for all the approaches were blocked with long confused lines of those seeking alms. The house was full of noise, and the clerks and monks were busy washing the feet of the people. Himself was seated in the midst on his bishop's stool, worn out with toil, yet fain to be saying the psalms, if he might no longer take his part in the washing. Meanwhile his heart was full of pity, desiring that all should be satisfied and none go away empty. And now once and twice all had departed gladdened with gifts of raiment and money and shoes, and with bellies well filled. But when a third great company of the poor was being set down, a monk whispered to the Bishop that money and garments were all spent, and that there was but little food left, the steward and the chamberlains could find no more. What did it profit to wash men's feet if there was naught to give them when they were washed? Nay, said the Bishop, let the Lord's will be done. His bounty will not fail to find meat for his servants. My servants will not do my will? They shall be fain to do it when I am taken from them. Scarcely had he spoken these words when there entered three messengers treading one upon another's heels in their haste. The first cried that he had brought money, the second a horse, the third a gift of oxen. Wulstan lifted eyes and hands to heaven rejoicing in the miracle, not so much for his own sake as that it was profitable to the poor. The monks wept for joy, and were right glad they had such a master. All men blessed God who would not bring to naught the prayers of them that trusted in Him, nor suffer Wulstan to be cast down even for an hour. So the horse and the oxen were sold, and the price of them with the money that had been brought in availed for alms to the needy.

CHAPTER XX

HE had forewarned his servants to make ready a choice banquet for that Easter, for that he was minded to dine with good men. They understood him not, and had bidden many men of substance. But when

Easterday was come he brought into the hall as many poor men as it would contain, and sitting among them bade set on the dinner. Thereat his steward was exceeding wroth, and wounded the Bishop's gentle heart with bitter murmuring: saying it was more fitting that the Bishop should dine with a small company of rich men than with a great company of poor. To that he answered, They are rich who know the will of God and can do it. Them we must serve who have naught to repay us withal. God will repay since the needy cannot bid us in turn to feasts. For me it is more joyful to behold this company than if I were, as I often have been, sitting down with the King of England. For, as I have said the King and his nobles did greatly honour Wulstan, and bade him to their tables, and respected his counsel, yea, especially those who followed after justice. For to some men it comes by nature to admire in others what they cannot themselves hope to attain. What do I say regarding the magnates of England? The Kings of Ireland paid him many signs of reverence. Malcolm, King of Scotland, with his royal lady Margaret, commended himself to his prayers. The fame of his holiness had gone through all the land, and even to the ends of the world. The Pope of Rome, the Archbishop of Bari, the Patriarch of Jerusalem, in letters which are extant, besought his advocacy with God. Indeed there was no earthly glory that did not pursue him while he shunned it and refused it. There was, as it were, a strife between the man and glory. The more earnestly he fled from it, the more steadily did it pursue him. But of such matters let me have said thus much and no more, while I tremble to speak of his departure from this world whereat there was weeping on earth, joy in heaven. For now that I am to speak with what poor skill I may, I beseech thee, Lord Christ, that I may be enabled so to tell of Thy gifts in him, as may be pleasing to Thee, to him not unpleasing. For Thine, O Lord, are the graces that we praise in Wulstan, seeing that all our life is Thine. Wherefore I seek with all my heart Thine almighty mercies, that Thou wilt accept this little book of mine, that I lose not the fruits of my poor labours.

CHAPTER XXI

AT the Pentecost next after that Easter, he was taken with a great weakness in all his members, and lay sick upon his bed. He bade his servants ride post to his friend Robert Bishop of Hereford and bid him come. Robert when he heard it was straightway with him. Wulstan made his confession of human frailties, and even received the discipline, for so the monks call being beaten with rods on the bare back. How great a man was this, who, when he was bowed with age and sickness, and at peace in his mind, yet did not withhold his body from the scourge, that he might be made clean of any stain that lay yet upon his spirit. From that time until the Circumcision of the Lord he seemed sometimes to be easier; sometimes he went to his bed again. A slow ever-present fever was carrying him to his end. The weakness of his body gave new vigour to his mind, as if the heat of the distemper could ripen in him whatever was not yet ready for eternal glory. After the Circumcision Bishop Robert, and the venerable Abbots Serlo of Gloucester and Gerald of Tewkesbury visited the sick man. There he absolved by his own right, after having confessed himself as was his wont: and bade them a last farewell. The sickness grew worse from day to day. Christ was making ready for him the departure which called him to heaven. Meanwhile he did not take holiday from the service of God—but, not forgetting his former zeal, would still be praying, often with his lips, always in his heart. Sitting rather than lying he gave his ears to the psalms, his eyes to the Altar, for his chair was so placed that he could freely see what was being done in the Chapel. Eight days before his death he received Holy Unction from Prior Thomas. Daily thereafter he received the Eucharist to carry him safe on his journey. He breathed forth his latest breath a little after midnight on Saturday the nineteenth day of January, in the year of the Incarnation of Our Lord one thousand and ninety-five, the eighth year of the reign of William II, when he had been Bishop for thirty-four years four months and thirteen days, and in about the eighty-seventh year of his age.

It is notable that he himself knew that he should live to a great age: for he foretold it often, and one day right pleasantly in Chapter. The brethren were sitting about him and talking of many things when he bowed his head and yielded to sleep. They all fell to wailing and lamenting, crying out that he would soon die and leave them comfortless. But when he woke and learned the cause of their trouble, he answered and said, Believe me as long as my old body can endure, I shall not die—nor shall this frame be dissolved but in extreme age. But when I shall have departed, I shall be the more present with you, and will let none of those whom ye fear hurt you, if ye are faithful servants of God.

CHAPTER XXII

SO they washed his body which shone with the hope of eternal resurrection, so that all marvelled and worshipped, for that it was bright like a jewel, pure and white as milk. Even his nose which in his life stood forth overmuch minished and grew white after his death, to the wonder of the beholders. Another thing that I will tell passed for a miracle with those who were standing by. The ring which he received at his consecration had often fallen off before this time. For many years before his death the flesh of his fingers was so wasted that the skin seemed scarce to cleave to the bones. So thin had his body become through old age, or as I would rather say, through fasting. So it came to pass that the ring often slipped, to the great sorrow of the monks who took it as a sign of the Bishop's approaching death. He was sorry for them and soothed them with the oil of gentle words. Put away sorrow from your brows, he said. The ring will be there when you look for it. It came to me unsought, and I will carry it to the grave. So it befell many times. The ring, often slipping off, was never wholly lost, but always found again. But now as I began to tell, some of them tried to draw the ring from his finger, whether to keep it as a relic, or to prove the truth of his promise. But try as they might they could not get it off and gave it up. The knotted joints and the unyielding skin and sinews mocked all their skill.

CHAPTER XXIII

MEANWHILE the corpse was made ready and carried into the Church which he himself had builded anew. The bier was set down before the Altar, the clerks sitting about it. All that night, and the day and night after their prayers and tears went up to God as the incense. At that time Bishop Robert of Hereford was at the King's Court, a man of much worldly prudence, but of virtuous life. At that same hour in which the Saint departed this life, Robert beheld him stand before him, much changed from the Wulstan he had known in latter years; for his countenance was youthful and ruddy and shone with light as of the stars. He was clad in the vestments of a bishop, holding his staff in his hand, and seemed thus to address the sleeper: Come now, dear brother Robert, to Worcester. I will that thou shalt, with due rites, commit my body to the ground, my soul to God. Robert seemed to answer: Dear lord and friend, dost thou bid me bury thee when I have not seen thee look so hale these five years? Be that as it may quoth Wulstan, such is the will of God which thou must perform. Go swiftly, and give heed unto my words. Then the Bishop, knowing that the vision spake truly, carried it to the King's ears. The King gave him leave, and Robert rode right swiftly across the broad lands that are between London and Worcester. The strength of holy friendship made light of the toilsome journey, that friendship which had bound him to Wulstan since the day he was made a bishop: and God so prospered his good will that he came to Worcester before the time appointed for the burial: for the monks had delayed it of set purpose, and awaited his coming. On this first night the spirit of Wulstan called his friend Robert lying far away, to bear his part in the burying of him.

Next night, as if he had come home from a journey, he showed many wondrous things to them at Worcester. Some of the monks, wearied out with long watching had crept off into corners to sleep at their ease where none could see them. But Wulstan was continually among them, stirring the sleepers, awaking the drowsy. Arise, he cried, put away slumber: repeat the psalter through: end with the commendation of the soul. They did even as he bade them, making a virtue of necessity. Seeing that they might not do what they would, they were fain to do what they might. There was one among them who meditated in his heart a wicked deed, but had not yet carried thought to act. To him the Saint appeared in great wrath, rebuking the guilty purpose; magnifying its wickedness, and sternly warning him against its accomplishment. There was sin enough and overmuch in the thought, let him therefore refrain from the act. If he hoped to be spared he must stay the deed: for he would swiftly be punished and die that same year if he did not hold back from that sin. The monk terrified by the Saint's threat, and by his own guilty conscience, promised that he would renounce his purpose, and henceforth be a faithful servant of the Rule.

CHAPTER XXIV

AND now came the Sunday of the burial. Bishop Robert had come in such hot haste that he had scarce breath to tell them of his vision. When Masses had been duly said, Robert committed the Saint's body to the grave. Then, as if none had mourned before, began a great weeping and wailing. The whole multitude burst into lamentations which echoed and re-echoed in the vaulted roof. Their tears of sorrow, manifold and from the heart, bore witness that Wulstan's death was the downfall of religion, a calamity to England. You could scarce tell which had deeper cause for grief, clergy or people; while they cried for their watchful shepherd, they for their master and teacher: young or old, these thinking wistfully on his ripeness, those on his kindness. The rich praised his sparing use of riches, the poor his bounteous charity. At last they committed the dear, dear father's bones to the tomb, but his memory was never put out of sight in their hearts. You scarce could find a convent or a city wherein reverence for a departed bishop was more tenderly, nay so tenderly cherished. So every week if a day had no proper service, and when the rolling year brought round his obit, the monks sang psalms and Masses, the citizens were lavish in almsgiving. He himself freely granted the petitions of them that entreated him—and there was none who sought him in faith but gained the boon of his intercession.

i

CHAPTER XXV

I WILL make known two instances to show that not even in little things did he suffer them that loved him to be vexed. Soon after his death a book which they call an epistoler was stolen from the Church. The sacrist who had charge of it was blamed. The Prior raged at him and threatened him with a grievous penance if the book were not given back. The monk sought for it everywhere, but in vain: and at last betook him to the intercession of the Saint—whose known kindness of heart made him hope that his prayers would not be wasted. So he lay on his face at Wulstan's tomb praying and beseeching him to bethink him of his kindness in former days, and cause the book to be restored, and silence the threats of the Prior. He bargained moreover that in return he would burn a candle for a whole year at the tomb, and say fifteen psalms. That day there was busy search and questioning among the people—and behold, before evening the book was given back. A woman accused the thief and showed where the book was hidden.

CHAPTER XXVI

ABOUT the same time a lay servant of the Church, who had often been employed by the sacrist and found honest, complained that a book had been stolen from him. He was the more troubled because it was borrowed, and the owner was pressing him to return it. Therefore every day he cast himself down at Wulstan's tomb and prayed to God that for the merits of the Bishop He would bring back the book and punish the greedy thief. If his prayer was granted he would be careful henceforth to pay faithful service to the Church. Days passed: and he continued instant in prayer. On the day of the Ascension he prayed longer and more earnestly than he was wont. And at dusk the guilty person dared to profane the House of God by entering it. The servant ceased not from prayer, and the thief, suddenly seized with devilish madness, began to raise frightful screams. Nay more, he plucked the stolen book from his bosom, and showed it, and declared when and in what manner he had stolen it. So the robber lost his wits, and the man that prayed got back what he had lost. But the brother of the sufferer, who was a monk of the House, a ready and prudent man, soon persuaded the brethren to beseech the gentleness of the Saint that he would restore the madman to a sound mind. This they did with good will and anon obtained their petition. It came to be a custom among the Worcester monks that if they ailed at all in body or were troubled in mind they whispered it to the Bishop just as though he were still alive. He received the prayers of all in the large lap of his charity, and granted so many of their petitions, that I believe if any went away unsatisfied, it was not that the Saint could not, but that the man who asked was unworthy, or the thing asked was unnecessary.

CHAPTER XXVII

MANY were cheered in sleep by dreams of his glory—many comforted with open visions by day: whereof it is enough to make mention of a few. There was a certain enclosed servant of God, given to prayer and solitude as is the way of anchorites. The Old Enemy who could not take away his religion from him grudged him his peace, and devised grievous vexations for him. The wicked spirit strove mightily so that not for a day, nay, not for an hour, did his crafty attacks cease. The good hermit could be wearied: he could not be conquered; for God's help can prevail when human weakness fails. The conflict was brought to an end by the prayers of the most holy Bishop; and an inner garment which he had worn when he lay dying was sent from Worcester. A strange thing and worthy of reverence followed. So soon as the anchorite received the garment, nay as soon as he beheld it, the clouds that beset him fled, and peace of mind returned. Thereafter he felt no more temptations or evil suggestions. Wherefore perceiving that his merits were far below the holiness of Wulstan he reverenced the garment as a relic. He folded it carefully, and when he was minded to sleep laid it over his head to guard him from all the deceiving shows of the enemy.

CHAPTER XXVIII

ONE day when the sun was about setting, the same hermit was alarmed by loud knocking at his window, and asked who it might be. The answer came that his friend Wulstan Bishop of Worcester was without, and desired if he had water by him that he should bring it to wash his hands withal. His reward should be that he should go into the Church and say the hours for his friend. As a further pledge of friendship he should give him a cloak which he possessed. The anchorite replied that he had no such thing, and the Bishop well knew it—but Wulstan answered him with a promise that he should have it anon if he would fix his mind on God. Such a bright light shone as it seemed from the appearance of the Bishop's body that it touched all things about it with its radiance. Then he went into the Church, genuflected, said a prayer, and crossed himself and began the Office of the Hours. The responses were taken up by three maidens who were a marvel of beauty and grace. When they had finished chanting, the tallest maiden who was in the midst gave a blessing to the Bishop who received it. Meanwhile, the solitary thought he beheld a bed nobly furnished and a cloak spread thereon, and when he bade the Bishop accept what he had asked, he received this answer, that he should have hereafter by grace a pledge of greater glory. He bade him moreover to carry his most loving greetings to the men of Worcester. He thanked them in his heart for that they had so long watched in prayer. All their prayers and watching availed for their own good for all they thought to do for Wulstan should return unto their own bosom. Then the vision passed—and the servant of God told it next day faithfully.

The monks were faithful to their duty—letters were sent throughout England to tell of their sorrow, and testifying to their love. Men asked concerning him as if God Himself were to inform a man of something that concerned his salvation and fulfil the prayers of them that eagerly desired with good news. There was at this time at Brumeton a priest of good life named Dunstan; I remember having heard as a boy of the sweet savour of his holiness. Like unto him in the pursuit of virtue an anchoress of the same town watched with him; one who fell behind no man in holiness. I know not which you would set above the other, so evenly matched were they in the race for goodness; the priest in the work of instruction, the woman in the discipline of obedience. They were persons notable in religion whom God deemed worthy of the heavenly vision while they yet were in this life. They sent to the men of Worcester and bade them have no doubts of the good estate of Wulstan; for they had seen him in the choirs of the saints no less glorious than his fellows, and indeed somewhat more glorious than certain of the lower rank. Any man who will not believe their word offends against religion which they did so steadfastly cherish that there is nothing more excellent especially in our days. Indeed whatever they said was received as if it came from the heavenly temple and echoed through the holy of holies.

Methinks I have performed your bidding, my lords and fathers, in setting down with my poor pen the life of a most holy man. I have shown my obedience even if I have not fulfilled your hopes. Ye are judges whether I have done both. My good will pleads for my infirmity: for if I could not do what I ought, I have done what I could. Let me claim therefore your lasting favour for my little labour, seeing that I have given near six weeks to doing your will and pleasure. It will be but just therefore that when my soul shall have departed from this body, ye shall offer Masses unto God for me on as many days as I have spent nights in watching for Wulstan's sake. Farewell.

Here ends the Life of S. Wulstan, Bishop and Confessor, whose holy deposition is kept on the nineteenth day of January.

Also publlished by Llanerch:

AN AGE OF SAINTS
Chalwyn James

SYMBOLISM OF THE CELTIC CROSS
Derek Bryce

THE LIFE OF ST SAMSON OF DOL
Thomas Taylor

SAINT COLUMBA OF IONA
Lucy Menzies

LIVES OF THE SCOTTISH SAINTS
W. Metcalfe

LIVES OF THE NORTHUMBRIAN SAINTS
Sabine Baring-Gould

ANGLO-SAXON
RELIGIOUS VERSE ALLEGORIES
Louis Rodrigues

THE DARK AGE SAINTS OF SOMERSET
John Sea

BELOVED VALLEY:
THE LIFE OF ST. TEILO
Anne Lewis

For a complete list of **Llanerch Press Ltd** publications, please visit our website: www.llanerchpress.com or alternatively write to: **Llanerch Press Ltd** Little Court, 48 Rectory Road, Burnham-on-Sea, Somerset. TA8 2BZ